Praying
God's End-Time
Manifesto

To Robin
With Love
Ps. 92:13-15
(Amplified
Trans.)
2/17/21

NANCY BRASSFIELD

HIM
HARVEST INTERNATIONAL MINISTRIES

Published by:
Harvest International Ministries, Inc
333 County Road 320
Bertram, Texas 78605

Printed in the United States of America

Second Printing: 2019
ISBN: 9781092297066

TABLE OF CONTENTS

FOREWORD

Mama Nancy Brassfield has given her life to prayer. And finally, after years of carrying this around in the womb of her heart, the Lord has released her to write this book. The understanding the Lord has given her on prayer makes this a book you will use every day. She's done some incredible research on other Praying Mamas that have birthed prayer movements and changed the course of history.

Praying Mamas, God's End-Time Manifesto is a Clarion Call for intercessors everywhere, to go deeper in prayer. "Deep calling unto deep" (Psalm 42:7).

This book couldn't have come at a better time. The body of Christ needs these truths right now, more than any other time in the history of the Church. She didn't write a "THIS IS HOW I DO IT" book. She has written a book full of scriptures from God's Word. She tells us how we must be engaged and how to be intentional about our prayer life; a life given to ministering unto the Lord but also partnering with Heaven in taking out the enemy over our families, our friends, our cities, our state and our nation. I pray that this book will encourage you the same way it has me.

My mama prayed for her family as long as she lived on Earth. If Jesus is doing intercession for us, the saints, according to Hebrews 7:25, I believe my mama is right there praying with Him. She loved to pray. Mama was saved when she was six years old at a revival meeting in an old Freewill Baptist Church at Cordell, KY.

She told me about it many times when I was growing up. She would tell me about going down to the altar to pray and asking Jesus to forgive her sins and come into her heart and save her. Even in her older years, her precious blue eyes would get full of tears and run down her cheeks just talking about it. She was still so thankful for the Savior's love and saving grace.

That altar moment when she gave her life to Jesus was still fresh in her heart. It never left her. Tenderness and humility were two keys to her prayer life. I believe thankfulness and praise are also keys to being effective in prayer. It's like the two wings of an eagle. In order for it to fly properly, both wings have to be working together. Thankfulness and praise bring prayer and proclamation. We enter the door through thankfulness, and we approach Him through praise and worship.

> Enter his gates with thanksgiving and into His courts with praise; give thanks to Him and praise His Name.   Psalm 100:4

Many people pray from the outer courts. They don't realize that when Jesus paid for our sins, He gave us access into the throne room of God the Father. That's where true intimacy begins.

My mama never called herself an intercessor; I don't think she even knew what that word meant. She just knew that if she was faithful to pray, God would be faithful to answer. She believed Luke 11:9-10, "Ask, seek and knock!" Me, my sister and two brothers put Mama and Daddy through a lot of pain and sorrow in our early years, but they kept right on praying and loving us.

That's what Praying Mamas and Daddys do. No way in this world could I have made it without their prayers. We must have greater love in our heart to be effective in prayer. The greater the love, the deeper we can go!

> Confess your trespasses to one another, and pray for one another, that you may be healed. The effective, fervent prayer of a righteous man (and woman) avails much.

James 5:16, NKJV

My mama knew something vitally important about prayer. She called it "faith-believing." She would say, "Now honey, you've got to pray with faith-believing." I didn't know it then, but now I would call that praying with "believing-faith." That's praying with a purpose, seeing it before you pray for it, having a goal in mind. Don't give up on your vision; stay with it. Ask the Lord to keep showing you the vision until you see the fruit from it.

We should be as confident in prayer as we are when we turn on a light switch in our living room. We know as soon as we act and flip that switch, the light is gonna come on. If it doesn't, then there is a break in the connection. We can also have a break in our connection with the Holy Spirit. We can offend Him by believing someone else's word over His. That truly breaks His heart. If the Lord said it, He means it, and we must believe it. He wants us to really take Him at His Word! Jesus said, "Only believe." His Word is our survival kit in this wilderness of prayer. Ask the Lord to increase your faith. I've had to many times in my own journey.

So when we pray, we should always ask the Lord if we've offended Him in any way so that we can repent, get clean of the offense, and receive the forgiveness that's promised us if we confess our sins, so that there will be nothing between us and the Lord when we pray.

King David was a big sinner, but he was also quick to repent. And that kept him in good standing with the Lord. So when we know we've sinned, go to the Lord quickly and humbly. He already knows what you're coming for, and what you did. He wants to hear you confess it, so that He can be released to do what His Word says He will do. He's always proving Himself by His Word.

Charles Spurgeon once said: "A Bible that's falling apart, probably belongs to someone who isn't!" Read your Bible; devour your Bible. The Word of God is the key that opens the doorway to prayer and His presence. When Jesus is knocking at the door, that's what He means by:

> Listen! I stand at the door and knock. If anyone hears My voice and (opens) the door, I will come in to him and have dinner with him, and he with Me.
> Revelation 3:20, HCSB

When we open the door to Him, He brings the Bread and the Wine with Him. Sounds like some feasting is fixing to happen, feasting on the Word, with the Word. He is the Word, and He is the Bread of Life. His blood is the Wine. We eat the Bread; we sip the Wine; we listen; then we get a revelation of who He is. It's all about relationship. That's where effective prayer happens, knowing who He is in us. Trusting in His abilities, not dwelling on our inabilities! We've got to get rid of our stinkin' thinkin'.

See Proverbs 23:7, Matthew 12:34. We must start seeing ourselves the way Jesus sees us. You may feel like a third-class citizen here, but I can tell you, feelings have nothing to do with faith. If you're a blood bought child of the King, you're a first-class citizen of Heaven. That ought to settle it, now and forever. You need to tell the devil that's who you are, that's who he's dealing with, that's who he's lying to, who he's accusing, and you need to say it out loud so he can hear it. He can't read your mind, but he can sure hear what comes out of your mouth, believe me, he uses every negative word you say about yourself, so don't let him get away with it. Jesus said in John 8:44: "He is liar, and the father of it."

John the Baptist told the large crowd that was waiting to be baptized by him, "I indeed baptize you with water unto repentance, but there's one coming after me who's mightier than I, whose sandals I'm not worthy to carry, He will baptize you with the Holy Ghost and Fire."
Matthew 3:11

He that believeth on me, as the scripture hath said, out of his belly shall flow rivers of living water.
John 7:38, KJV

We want the Word of God to come out of us like a fire hose, not to put out a fire, but to start one; the fires of revival. Let's be Spirit Filled fire hoses, starting fires in our friends, our families, our workplaces, and our churches. Every revival in history was started through someone who was hungry for the Word of God, and hungry to pray! They didn't just live to pray; they prayed to live!

Lord Jesus, create in us a hunger to pray like we've never prayed before. Never in our history Lord has there been a time like we're in right now. I know You are praying; your Word says you are. Help us to pray without ceasing like you're praying Lord. Amen.

We need fresh eyes and ears today especially you young sisters that are just getting started in marriage, or maybe you have some little ones already. Your marriage and your children are your first and most important mission field, and you'll be on the battle lines in this war for many years to come. The devil hates you; he hates your husband; he hates your children; he hates everything about you because you've chosen Jesus over him. He will use every weapon in his arsenal to try and defeat you and keep you from becoming the Praying Mama you were called to be.

They overcame him by the Blood of The Lamb and the word of their testimony, and they did not love their lives to the death.   Revelation 12:11

In Revelation 5:6, the Apostle John saw Jesus in Heaven and said: "I saw One like a slaughtered lamb standing."

This says to me, "He is standing up for us, His blood is still flowing, His Word is still alive, and His promises are still available for those who believe."

Don't forget to pray by the blood of Jesus; cover your family in the blood. It's still fresh and full of power and might. Remember, you and Jesus are a majority at any time, in any situation! And don't you forget that you have the strongest and most powerful weapon in the universe, the Weapon Of Prayer.

We don't have to be a soldier in a uniform
To be of service over there
While the soldiers bravely stand
With the weapons made by hand
Let us trust and use The Weapon Of Prayer.[1]

Mama Nancy is connecting the dots. She's weaving and sewing the patches of scripture together to make a beautiful quilt, or a Joseph's coat; a coat of His Love to cover us in this time of great turmoil. The greatest opportunity the Church has ever had to really rise up and be the Church of the living God is now, not tomorrow not next week or next year. Now is the time, today is the day. **Come on Praying Mamas; We're not gonna make it without you!**

Ricky Skaggs ♭♪

New Country Music Hall of Fame Voices in the Hall Podcast, https://www.rickyskaggs.com. Accessed March 8, 2019

---

[1] From the song: *Weapon Of Prayer* by the Louvin Brothers.

INTRODUCTION

Where There's a Praying Mother, There's Always Hope.
— J. C. Rye

I shall never forget that Sunday morning in 1995. I awakened early in order to have my time with the Lord before going to church. In retrospect, nothing was unusual about that particular day; however, it turned out to be one of those defining moments in my life of which I will always remember. I still look back on the events that transpired. The happenings have left an indelible imprint upon my mind.

During my prayer time, the Holy Spirit spoke these words to me. "Today I am extending to you my scepter of authority." The utterance wasn't an audible voice, capable of being heard by others, but to me it was loud, clear and to the point. Suddenly, in a moment's time, my spiritual eyes and ears were opened; I experienced a Divine encounter that awakened me to my prophetic destiny.

I was running late, so there wasn't enough time for me to process what was spoken to me, but I was cognizant of the fact that I needed to take it seriously.

When I arrived at church, nothing seemed out of the ordinary. The praise team was getting ready for worship, and the atmosphere was filled with great anticipation. People were arriving, excited about our guest speaker; we had anticipated his coming for a long time. We had our usual meet and greet time. My thoughts were something like this, "No pressure for me today, just sit and enjoy."

Worship was exceptionally good, and the Presence was certainly in the midst of the gathering. As I sat down, ready for the service to transition, my thought processes and my whole being were suddenly invaded by Holy Spirit. I was not expecting that kind of visitation. I am familiar with the Voice of God, but this was definitely different. When He spoke, it was as if we were talking face to face. It was very precise, clear and to the point.

First, He said:

> In the last days I am going to restore women back to their purpose and position alongside men. It will be as it was in beginning.
>
> Genesis 1:27-28

Secondly, He said:

> In the last days, my people will need to reside in Psalm 91. You are to teach both men and women to dwell in the secret place of the Most High and how to appropriate the promises of divine protection and deliverance found in that chapter of the Psalms.

It was the same voice of the Spirit I heard earlier that morning when He spoke to me about His scepter of authority, and now He had just given me a mandate for future generations. All the ramifications of what The Father spoke to me were still a little vague. I did understand that a scepter was an emblem of authority and the Word of God says we have a scepter of strength from Zion and we are to rule in midst of our foes (Psalm 110).

Our speaker was the amplified version and taught from Genesis to Revelations. He had a great sense of humor that he interjected into his teaching. I know this sounds rude, but I just wanted him to get through so I could share with the people what Holy Spirit had spoken to me.

Understand, I rarely spoke in the church services, much less get up when we had a renowned speaker known for his expertise in expounding the Word of God. I can recall to this day the excitement I felt; it was difficult to contain my emotions. Usually, I would rationalize and come to the conclusion, *It might be better to wait until another time to share my experience and not let my emotions over rule my ability to think rationally.* However, that was not the case this particular day. I had a Word from the Lord and I wanted to share it with the congregation, especially the women. Perhaps my zeal did overpower my wisdom but as a result of my sharing, I received valuable revelation that would unlock one of the secrets of spiritual growth and maturity, *The Importance of Dwelling in His Presence.*

It seemed an eternity before our guest finished and turned the service back to my husband. Perceiving it was the proper time, I asked to share with the congregation the encounter I experienced earlier that morning. I spoke as briefly as possible. Suddenly, right in front of God, our guest and all those people, I requested to bring the message the following Sunday morning. Perhaps my husband was in shock; He graciously gave me permission. What was he to do, say no in front of everyone? I am grateful he trusted me enough to say yes.

After the benediction, with enthusiasm, people began to gather around me. The women were especially exuberant because a portion of the word related to them personally. When the excitement of the service had subsided and most of the people had left the sanctuary, I noticed the speaker coming towards me. I didn't want to be presumptuous, but my superwoman confidence was slowly waning. My thought was, *Perhaps he is coming to encourage me.* His words of affirmation would certainly boost my confidence to complete the assignment God had given me.

Instead of affirming me, he spoke to me briefly and said, "I felt led to give you this book." "It is my personal copy of *The Secret of the Stairs*, given to me by Wade Taylor, the author." To this day, I am thankful he didn't boost my ego with words of encouragement. His accolades would have been short lived, but the treasure he gave me will live eternally.

The message in the book, *The Secret of the Stairs*[1], is directed toward those who actively desire to come into the fullness of all our Lord desires for them; those who are spiritually hungry and identify with the heart cry of the Apostle Paul: "That I may know Him" (Philippians 3:1).

I suppose he discerned I had a lot of zeal but needed some spiritual maturity before I could successfully finish the mandate Father had given me. I think he was right.

May I be a little facetious here? *What was I thinking?* Before I processed the events of that day, I was enamored with the thought of receiving a scepter that represented the King's authority. Perhaps, like Queen Esther of old, I was favored by the King. I love prophetic acts, symbolic actions in the earthly realm, release a power shift in the Spirit realm. I could hardly wait to locate one of those infamous bling stores that sell crowns and scepters. My thoughts were honorable. I could buy a scepter, it would be a great tool for prophetic acts, and a constant reminder of my prophetic destiny.

Later, when I began to research the meaning of mandates and scepters of authority, it didn't seem quite as intriguing as it was that Sunday morning in my war room. How naive could I be? Scepters and authority had a different connotation than I perceived. Some warfare would certainly be involved when using my new scepter. *Was I ready for that level of warfare? Sad to say, I think not.*

---

[1] Taylor, Wade E. (2013-11-01). The Secret of the Stairs (Kindle Locations 90-91). Advanced Global Publishing. Kindle

Praying Mama, if you get nothing out of this book but the following statement, you will have gained some much needed wisdom. My husband coined this phrase:

Charisma without character will kill you and those around you.

What a disaster it would have been for me to go to war with the King's scepter without knowing His character and an intimate knowledge of Him and His ways. The Father desires a relationship with us. I was so busy doing for Him; I let being in His Presence become secondary in my life.

In his book, *Practicing His Presence*, Brother Lawrence wrote this, "We used to sing a song in the church in Benton which I like, but which I never really practiced until now." It runs:

> Moment by moment I'm kept in His love;
> Moment by moment I've life from above;
> Looking to Jesus till glory doth shine;
> Moment by moment, O Lord, I am thine.[1]

It is exactly that "moment by moment," every waking moment, surrender, responsiveness, obedience, sensitiveness, pliability, lost in His love, that I now have the mindset to explore with all my might, to respond to Jesus Christ as a violin responds to the bow of the master.

A few years ago, my husband and I were attending a prophetic conference. A nationally known prophet prophesied over me. He spoke some encouraging words that brought edification and confirmation to me. Then, he dropped the bomb. He said, "You need to write. Heaven doesn't need your knowledge. Earth does."

---

[1] Lawrence & Frank Lauback, Edition. Practicing His Presence, Brother Lawrence & Frank Lauback. Seed Sowers Publishing, P.O. Box 3317, Jacksonville, FL 32206.

I had a brief moment of cynicism thinking, *Me write, what could I possibly write that hasn't already been written, why another book?*

However, as a result of that prophetic word, I am penning this book.

Feeling inadequate about my writing ability, I went to God's Word for encouragement and read as follows:

> Trust in the Eternal One, your True God, not in your own abilities, and you will be supported. Put your trust in His words that you heard through the prophets, and you will succeed.
>
> 2 Chronicles 20:20, The Voice Bible (paraphrase mine)

When I began the quest for a book title, I knew without doubt the church had entered a new era, and women are on the front burner in God's end-time plan of restoration. Many have referred to this new era as an Era of Conquest. I am convinced that in this era, a new breed of warriors will arise with a conquering spirit, ready for battle. I like to refer to these warriors as Praying Mamas. These new warriors possess both a warring spirit, and a heart that only a mother can have for her children.

It is my desire, by the time you finish reading this book that you will have experienced a personal encounter with God and feel invigorated, empowered, and equipped to seize a crippled generation from the hands of a cruel enemy.

Satan's plan has always been to control and destroy our children. Vladimir Lenin, founder of the Russian Communist Party said, "Give me just one generation of youth, and I'll transform the whole world.[1]"

---

[1] Vladimir Lenin, https://www.goodreads.com/quotes/106700-give-me-just-one-generation-of-youth-and-i-ll-transform.

Adolf Hitler made no bones about it. His philosophy was:

"He alone, who owns the youth, gains the future.[1]*"*

We war against an enemy that has already been defeated. Perhaps some of you may have concluded that it is too late for your tribe; they are too messed up. I can only tell you by experience, "It is never too late to start over."

It has been said, "If you aren't happy with yesterday, start anew today." All we need to do is take a step of faith and declare the promises God has decreed for our families.

Mothers, you have been in training for such a time as this, to be a voice to the next generation. God is looking for committed mothers, truly committed mothers who will be a part of the new prayer movement dedicated to the task of taking the Family Mountain and advancing the Kingdom of God upon the earth. Praying Mamas, you are **God's End-Time Manifesto.**

I conclude with this recent prophetic word concerning mothers:

Warrior mothers are arising. Warrior mothers are arising, fighting for their children in their prayers. Warrior mothers who are standing in the One who fights for them and their children, and the mothers have and are paving the way for some of the greatest demonstrations of His breakthrough and supernatural restoration and healing to the children they love, care for and future.[2]

---

[1] Adolf Hitler https://www.brainyquote.com/quotes/adolf_hitler_378177.
[2] Mothers Are Arising!! September 3, 2015, Lana Vawser, https://lanavawser.com/2015/09/03/mothers-are-arising.

ENDORSEMENTS

Nancy Brassfield has provided a great blessing to mothers throughout the Church world. This is the most inspiring and enlightening book I have ever read for Christian mothers. Any Mother who reads this book will be inspired to become a Praying Mama. They will be able to determine the destiny of their children. Nancy gives many illustrations.

Every Christian mother should read this book. It covers many more truths than the title portrays. Having 65 years of ministry, I can honestly say Nancy Brassfield has made a valuable contribution to the Body of Christ.

Bishop Bill Hamon
Christian International Apostolic-Global Network
Author: *The Eternal Church, Prophets & Personal Prophecy, Prophets & the Prophetic Movement, Prophets, Pitfalls, & Principles, Apostles/Prophets & the Coming Moves of God, The Day of the Saints, Who Am I & Why Am I here, Prophetic Scriptures Yet to be Fulfilled (3rd Reformation), 70 Reasons for Speaking in Tongues, and How Can These Things Be? God's Weapons of War*

Praying Mamas, by author Nancy Brassfield, is a true Spiritual Goldmine, just waiting to be explored, and the enormous wealth to be discovered. There is a rich Vein of Heavenly Gold that runs through the depths of this amazing book, from the first page and all the way through the last page. Reading it, I felt pulled in by the Holy Spirit to these profound hidden truths and treasures. Do not be fooled by the simple title, Praying Mamas. You will discover far more than you are expecting, for both men and women. Happy Mining!

Dr. Don Crum
President of Leadership International
Former Advisor to the White House, Washington, DC

We have known Nancy Brassfield for over 30 years. Nancy has had a profound impact upon those she has ministered to for many years. Indeed, she has touched our lives in countless ways, helping us to grow in our gifting and helping us through times of difficulty and sorrow. She is best defined as a quiet, but mighty and incredibly powerful warrior in the Lord. She has a quiet and demure physical presence but an anointed, powerful, and hugely effective presence in the Spiritual realm where the true battles rage.

Nancy's heart is to equip this generation with spiritual knowledge which is evident in her book, *Praying Mamas, God's End-Time Manifesto*. There is no one better to have on your side than a true spiritual warrior, and Nancy truly defines this.

Mark and Vangie Gregg
Co Founders: Simgenics Corporation
Grand Junction, Colorado
Author: *An Adventure With Princess Feathertree and Her Friends.*
Mark A. Gregg

Nancy's book, Praying Mamas is an encouraging, heartfelt, and very timely word in an era when mothering is often challenged by those who have to work outside the home, by those who agree to abortion, and by the changes in society, and the education our children experience today.

Her message to mothers is a must read. Mothers must build a strong relationship with the Lord. Make prayer a daily encounter with Him. If possible, this encounter with Him will give you authority, understanding, and wisdom to raise children who love you, who love God, and learn the power of answered prayers from Mamas. I love the proverb she included.

"The young bird does not crow until it hears the old ones".

Apostle Jim and Jean Hodges
President and Founders, FMCI

There are gifts given to us by God through people. In this beautifully written masterpiece we are enriched with loads of wealth concerning the powerful tools of prayer. Mama Nancy Brassfield's years of walking and talking with God is evident. It is an honor to read what she shares about our responsibility and God given power to declare God's word in the lives of every generation.

Pastors Gerald and Marketta Johnson
Faith Culture Church

Praying Mamas, God's End-time Manifesto is truly a commanding declaration for saving our children in today's world from the onslaught of internet trafficking. If you desire to protect and shield your children from the voice of the adversary, and you desire to know someone who has this burden, Nancy Brassfield's insights and testimonies will give you spiritual and practical wisdom from above. Get it, read it, and pass it on to your friends and loved ones. It can save your child from the powers of darkness. This resource is all about the saving prayers of our mamas and most importantly, you will learn the importance of speaking blessings over your offspring for generations to come.

Dr. Dennis G. Lindsay
President and Chief Executive Officer
Christ For The Nations, Inc.

We absolutely loved Mrs. Nancy's book! Not only is it written so well and so clear, but she has lived out and imparted its message to us over the past 16 years. As young people read the pages of this book, they will discover that age doesn't matter in order to be a mother or a father. All you need is a willing heart. It is with sincere joy that we recommend this outstanding book to you!

Rick and Lindsey Pino
Heart of David Movement

I am most certainly doing what I do today, to one degree or another, because of two "Praying Mamas," my mom and grandmother. I think there is an unwritten rule in Heaven: the prayers of moms take priority over all others! I can make no greater endorsement of this book than the following, "None is more qualified to write this book than Nancy Brassfield. READ IT!"

Dr. Dutch Sheets
Dutch Sheets Ministries
Colorado Springs, CO

A clarion call has been issued by Nancy Brassfield in her book, *Praying Mamas, God's End-Time Manifesto!* The manifesto is for women to arise with a warrior spirit and fight through intercession for their children, grandchildren and future generations.

Nancy describes the battle we are facing today as a battle of good versus evil. She gives vivid descriptions of winning the war by knowing God, knowing ourselves and then knowing your enemy. Receiving the anointing positions Praying Mamas to defeat the enemy at every difficult place.

I encourage every woman to pause, ponder and pray when reading this amazing book. Your life, the lives of your family members and the world will be a better place because of you as a Praying Mama!

Barbara Wentroble
President: International Breakthrough Ministries (IbM)
President: Breakthrough Business Leaders (BBL)
Author: *Prophetic Intercession; Praying with Authority; Council Room of the Lord (series); Fighting for Your Prophetic Promises*

Praying Mamas is the one of the sweetest and most powerful books that I have read.

It blessed my "Mama's heart so much and encouraged me to pray for my children and grandchildren! You will love it!

Dr. Cindy Jacobs
Generals International

PROLOGUE

No man is poor who has a godly mother.

— Abraham Lincoln

In a tribute to his late grandmother, our friend Doctor Eric Allerkamp, said this about the plans and purposes we step into. I quote him as saying:

"Remember that the plans and purposes of God that you step into today is not just about you. It is about your children and their children."

Praying Mamas, life is not *Que Sera, Sera, Whatever Will Be Will Be,* as the lyrics of the popular song from the fifties communicated in that era. The story in song went like this:

A little girl asked her mother what she would be. Her mother answered her with these words, "Que sera, sera, whatever will be, will be, the future's not ours to see, que sera, sera."

Que Sera, Sera, was an award winning pop song made popular by Doris Day, a legendary actress and singer. It was a fun song but probably led hundreds of thousands down the wrong path into their futures.

I am not suggesting that we are going to know all about our future and the future of our upcoming generations. However, I am proposing that you can help mold the future of your children through the avenue of prayer and declaring blessings over them. Corrie Ten Boom asked the question:

"Is prayer your steering wheel or your spare tire?"

It is a fact that a spare tire is no good to an automobile without a steering wheel to set the vehicle on course. The effectual, fervent prayer of a godly mother avails much and has the ability to shape a generation. Prayer must be a Mama's steering wheel for her family, not a spare tire.

February 28, 2018, President Trump and congressional leaders praised Billy Graham as America's pastor during a private ceremony at the U.S. Capitol. I listened very intently as the President delivered his eulogy about Reverend Graham. Many accolades were given, but the first couple of paragraphs are what caught my attention:

> In the spring of 1934, Billy Graham's father allowed a group of Charlotte businessmen to use a portion of the family's dairy farm to gather for a day of prayer. On that day, the men prayed for the city. They prayed that out of Charlotte the Lord would raise up someone to preach the Gospel to the ends of Earth.
>
> We are here today more than 80 years later because that prayer was truly answered. Billy Graham was 15 years old at the time. Just a few months later he accepted Jesus Christ as his Lord and Savior.
>
> That choice didn't just change Billy's life, it changed our lives. It changed our country and it changed, in fact, the entire world. The North Carolina farm boy walked out of those fields into a great and beautiful history.
>
> Starting at a small Bible school in Florida, he soon led a nationwide revival, from a large tent in Los Angeles, to 100,000 people in a single day at Yankee Stadium, to more than 2 million people at Madison Square Garden over 16 weeks in 1957. And, I remember that because my father said to me, "Come on son," and by the way, he said, "Come on, Mom. Let's go see Billy Graham at Yankee Stadium."

And it was something very special. But Americans came in droves to hear that great, young preacher. Fred Trump was a big fan. Fred Trump was my father. And like the faithful of Charlotte once did, today we say a prayer for our country that all across this land the Lord will raise up men and women like Billy Graham to spread a message of love and hope to every precious child of God.[1]

Praying Mama, can you, in your mind's eye, see the possibility of one of your own reaching millions for Jesus through the preaching of the gospel? Those people in Charlotte simply asked that God raise up someone from their community to carry the gospel to the ends of Earth. God heard their prayer and raised up a young 15-year-old farm boy to carry the good news to the nations. God is no respecter of persons; if He did it once, He will do it again. We just need to ask. You have been given the authority to declare great things over your children, community and nation. What are we waiting for? We are the ones He has been waiting for.

Can we agree with the prayer of a young college student as he knelt to pray in the room where John Wesley prayed? His prayer was not complicated, it was simple and to the point, *O Lord, do it again!*

In 1940, Dr. J. Edwin Orr took a group of Wheaton College students to study abroad in England. One of their stops included the Epworth Rectory. The rectory now serves as a Methodist museum, but it was the home of John Wesley, the founder of the Methodist movement. In one of the bedrooms, there are two impressions where it is believed that John Wesley regularly knelt in prayer. As the students were getting back on the bus, Dr. Orr noticed that one student was missing. Going back upstairs, Dr. Orr found a young Billy Graham kneeling in those kneeholes and praying, *O Lord, do it again!*[2]

[1] https://thehill.com/homenews/administration/376030-read-trumps-remarks-at-billy-graham-memorial-service. Accessed March 9, 2019.
[2] Mark Batterson, *Mark. Whisper*, The Crown Publishing Group. Kindle Edition, p 39.

Praying Mamas, in God's end-time manifesto he proclaimed that your sons and daughters would be filled with the Holy Spirit and would prophesy. He declared the Holy Spirit would be poured out on all flesh. Mama, you are flesh. Not only will your sons and daughters be infused with power, but it is also coming upon you in a double-portion measure. It is my prayer that as you read this book you will be determined that the enemy (Satan) cannot have another one of our children. Our prayer over our children can be as simple as O Lord, do it again; use my child to preach the gospel to the nations of the World.

I encourage you with this portion of a prophetic declaration given by Prophet Bill Yount, *I Am Awakening Your Children and Grandchildren:*

> The enemy is about to hear from our children and grandchildren, beginning this season. Watch and expect the passion for Christ to run wild like a raging fire inside of them. The Lord has allowed them to be placed in strategic locations on Earth, even in some unusual places where we think they shouldn't be, held in Satan's grip.
>
> They have now been divinely positioned to become a firebrand in God's hand to ignite and explode like dynamite inside the camp of the enemy! This is why the enemy forever has fought against marriages. He feared concerning the godly seed that was about to come upon Earth to do him in. And here they come![1]

Your descendants will defeat their enemies.
Genesis 22:17, MSG

---

[1] https://www.charismamag.com/blogs/prophetic-insight/33603-prophetic-vision-of-angelic-assignments-promises-multigenerational-blessings-for-praying-moms. Accessed March 9, 2019.

ACKNOWLEDGEMENTS

For out of him,
the sustainer of everything,
came everything,
and now everything
finds fulfillment in him.
May all praise and honor be given to him forever! Amen!

This book exists with grateful thanks to:

My dear husband Samuel for spurring me on when I wanted to give up. You wouldn't let me. You have always been the linchpin in my life; you listened faithfully to my long hours of whining while I was writing this book. Knowing you were up praying for me during the "222" night watch, gave me the courage to persevere to the finish line.

My two daughters, Vanessa and Suzanne, I acknowledge the two of you for teaching me on the journey of becoming a PRAYING MAMA. However, the two of you switched roles with me during the endeavor of writing this book. You became my PRAYING MAMAS in order for me to complete this manuscript. Your prods were sometimes painful, but you wouldn't let me quit. I am proud to be called your mother and friend.

Dana Marie Diaz, you are beautiful, both inside and out. I had a visual in mind of what I wanted my book cover to look like. I knew of no other person but you who could bring that image into fruition. You are a talented and beautiful artist. Your artwork depicted exactly the physical beauty of the next generation of Praying Mamas, messy buns and all that I was looking for. I am honored to have your fingerprints on my book. Thank you so much! You are destined for greatness in the Kingdom of God. Your gift of worship will have a lasting effect upon the next generation who seek after His Presence.

Sherry Williams, you came to my rescue just in time. You were the wind beneath my wings when you came along side to help me. Thank you for your expertise and gentle hand when there were corrections to be made. You were fair but firm.

Robert Luebke, I am grateful for your brilliant brain in the field of technology. You saved both me and my computer when I was ready to ditch the whole project because I couldn't make a PDF file and send an e-mail. Your research and expertise have been invaluable, and I am grateful you committed to see me through until the end. I learned quickly, it takes a tribe to get a book published. I am grateful you are part of my book writing tribe.

To my grandchildren Jacob and Destiny Myer and Admyer Studios, thank you for believing in me and providing the finances needed to publish this book. You planted seeds of encouragement and funds into this project, when you desperately needed encouragement of your own. You both are very talented and will get Jesus Kudos for every Praying Mama who reads this book and decides to war for this millennial generation of young people. Who knows, because of your financial gifts you may have helped pave the way for the next Billy Graham or John Wesley, who will win millions for the Kingdom of God. God's Blessings upon Admyer Studios and the beautiful work you do in the field of photography.

To my mother who at this moment is enjoying her eternal reward. Mama loved and prayed for her children, grandchildren, and great-grandchildren. She loved young people and did all she knew to do to be a mother to many. Her prayers are still alive and active. She was truly a Praying Mama. Thank you, mother, for praying for me, putting braces on my teeth, giving me piano lessons, and all the other things you did to push me into my Divine destiny.

To my friend, Norma Gorter, who faithfully worked with me getting this manuscript ready for the publisher. I never knew there were so many little things that make up the whole in book writing and publishing. Norma has a spirit of excellence and her sharp eye demands excellence. I am so grateful she prodded me to produce the best book possible for Kingdom purposes.

To my Faithful Friend, the Holy Spirit, who has been the constant stabilizer throughout my life. I could not have made it these 58 years without Him. I always felt I had at my personal disposal my very own counselor, comforter and friend whom I could rely on 24 hours a day, year after year. His knowledge is limitless and anything that is noteworthy in this book I credit to His infinite wisdom.

DEDICATION

I don't have to give much thought as to what my diamonds and pearls are. They are my two daughters, my grandchildren, great-grandchildren, and all the spiritual children God has so graciously entrusted to me throughout my time on Earth. They are my true treasures, and I love them all dearly and equally. However, I would like to dedicate this book, *Praying Mamas*, to my only biological granddaughter Jessica Denee' Hart.

Jessica is a prime example of the faithfulness of God. Her mother went into active labor in her first trimester and was told by a team of doctors that she had a slim chance of carrying her baby full term. She was flown by flight ambulance to Denver Children's Hospital, where a team of neonatal specialists was waiting her arrival, and quickly prepared for the delivery of a one-pound baby girl. The doctors said that if the baby was born this early and lived, it would have a very slim chance of a quality of life. Frightened and alone, my daughter, a young Praying Mama, cried aloud to her Heavenly Father, declaring His word that she would not give birth to her baby before its time. (Malachi 3:11, AMP).

Against all odds, that young Praying Mama carried her baby full term and birthed a beautiful and healthy baby girl named Jessica. The Hebrew meaning of the name Jessica is Rich and God Beholds. The University of Colorado still has the record of Jessica's birth on file because there was no logical answer as to the wonder that occurred that day. Yes, God beholds the cry of a Praying Mama.

I will give credit to whom credit is due. My granddaughter, Jessica, conceived and gave birth to the idea of a tribe of Praying Mamas several years ago. Her "Jessica Hart, FB video, January 2016", tells it all. Her passion was, and still is, to amass a tribe of Praying Mamas throughout her sphere of influence that would affect their community, the nation, and the world. Thinking her following would be between 50 to a 100, within a day, her tribe jumped to 800, then to 1500. Her words were,

> My heart is to band together a tribe of praying mothers who can laugh together, cry together, and speak encouragement and life into each other.

As she so uniquely shared, being a mother is tough and we all make mistakes. I don't feel qualified, but I am taking a leap of faith and launching this movement. Because of Jessica's promptings for me to write this book, her vision, and the heart cry of other young mothers, I knew it was time to for me to rise up as their Spiritual Doula, birth coach, and share what I have learned as a Praying Mama, grandmother, and great-grandmother.

Jessica, I dedicate this book to you and your dream of amassing many Praying Mama Tribes from around the world. As your grandmother, I admonish you to do more for the Kingdom of God than I ever thought of doing. Be very courageous and dare to be a mighty woman of God in your generation. Don't forget, you and other mothers just like you are God's Light in this dark world. Take this book, which now becomes your book, and gather your tribes together. You are fighting for your children's Divine destiny. ***If You Don't, Who Will?***

I love you dearly,
Nancy Brassfield, Grandma.

PREFACE

Only God Himself fully appreciates the influence of a Christian mother in the molding of character in her children.

— Billy Graham

Manifesto Defined

The word *manifesto* has taken a beating over the years. Because of the unusual nature of the word, I felt we needed a clear understanding of its meaning before we get into the content of this book.

When I was mandated by the Lord to write this book, Holy Spirit spoke two things to take into account for Praying Mamas. He said these empowered Mamas were to be the principal figures of this assignment, and they were to be the title feature. When I began to ponder a book title, I soon realized the words Praying Mamas, alone, did nothing dynamically for the composition. I concluded a more powerful subtitle was needed to give the book its much needed dynamics. Indecisively, I started to consider several seemingly good optional words and phrases, but nothing fit; I couldn't find the right combination. Over the years, *manifesto* was a word I was acquainted with, but it was not a term I used often.

I seriously began to entertain the word *manifesto* after hearing it used one morning on national news. The Breaking News that day was about a serial killer on the loose. His personal life and behaviors were highlighted, and they recounted all the horrendous murders he had committed. At the conclusion of the commentary, in disbelief, they read the following statement: "The killer left behind his written manifesto." That statement bellowed in my ears and was mind-altering for me. No matter how hard I tried, I could not get away from those two words, written manifesto.

When we use the word *manifesto*, it is understandable that immediately we think of either communists or some horrible, serial killer loose in a community. The 21st century news segment I alluded to above, certainly lends itself to the credence of our conception of the word.

From the Secular Perspective
According to the Merriam Webster's Collegiate Dictionary, plural manifestos or manifest:

> A written statement declaring publicly the intentions, motives, or views of its issuer. The group's manifesto focused on helping the poor and stopping violence.

Simply stated, a manifesto is a document that an organization or person writes that declares what is important to them and what they intend to do about it. It puts it all out there for people to grasp, ponder, and ultimately understand.

From a Biblical Standpoint
Perhaps the most famous manifesto of all time is the Bible which is also the most popular book ever written. The Sermon on the Mount, as found in Matthew 5-7, is probably the most clear and to the point statement of Jesus' teachings and can be likened to his manifesto concerning the Kingdom of God. He put it all out there for people to grasp and comprehend fully. I encourage you to read this sermon so you can better understand the manifesto.

My Personal Perspective
It is important to keep in mind, while manifestos are traditionally public declarations, anyone can have a personal manifesto.

I have always admired Dr. Martin Luther King. His *I Have a Dream* speech is widely regarded as the most famous manifestos and speeches ever given. Dr. King delivered his speech from the Lincoln Memorial to over 250,000 people on August 28, 1963. It was a pivotal moment in the U.S. Civil Rights Movement and also became a worldwide call for individuals to aspire to fulfilling their own dreams. I am still moved when I hear this historic manifesto declared by Dr. King!

The Benefits of a Manifesto
A manifesto will challenge the way you see things and encourage your commitment to change. If you feel inadequate about your abilities to be part of this last day move of God, most likely you need to write a personal manifesto. Your manifesto can be extremely useful because it becomes a constant source of inspiration to you and one that can be easily read every day. Let's face it, words, no matter how pretty and sweet they might be, don't really mean all that much if they don't prompt you to do something.

Allow me to use myself as an example. Never have I doubted the call of God to be a spokeswoman on His behalf. However, more often than not, I have pondered, *God Why Me?* Moses certainly was not over confident when God included him in His manifesto concerning freeing Israel from the savage cruelty of Egypt. The following is the dialogue between God and Moses found in Exodus 3-4:

GOD: The plea of Israel's children has come before Me, and I have observed the cruel treatment by the Egyptian's hands. So go. I'm sending you. I want you to gather My people, the children and bring them out of Egypt.

MOSES (to God): Who am I to confront Pharaoh and lead Israel's children out of Egypt?

MOSES (to God): Please Lord, I am not a talented speaker. I have never been good with words. I wasn't when I was younger, and I haven't gotten any better since You revealed Yourself to me. I stutter and stammer. My words get all twisted. Please, Lord, I beg you to send your message through someone else, anyone else.
Voice translation of the Bible, (emphases mine)

Like many of us, Moses continued to try and convince God that He had chosen the wrong person for the assignment. He contended with God that He should consider someone else who was more qualified. Praying Mama, can you identify with Moses' feelings of inadequacy when God instructed him to lead the children of Israel out of the cruel hands of Pharaoh's Egypt? I certainly can. We need to be aware of the enemy's strategy to keep our focus more on our inabilities, rather than our abilities through Christ.

Over the years I've tried to instill in my children, grandchildren, and now great-grandchildren that they can achieve anything through Christ. Philippians 4:13-14 is still their mainstay scripture. The Amplified version of these verses state it so clearly:

I can do all things [which He has called me to do] through Him who strengthens and empowers me [to fulfill His purpose--I am self-sufficient in Christ's sufficiency; I am ready for anything and equal to anything through Him who infuses me with inner strength and confident peace.]

Doesn't it give you a sense of security knowing God will never ask you to do anything without giving you the authority and the ability to accomplish it? He infuses us through the working of His Holy Spirit with that inner strength and power to get the job done.

I mentioned in the introduction of this book my encounter with God in the upper room of our home. I felt like Wonder Woman empowered by Holy Spirit, ready for anything. However, every time I got up to speak in a meeting, my Wonder Woman mentality quickly gave way to a grasshopper mentality especially if my husband and peers were present (Numbers 13). I would get dry mouthed, and my heart would feel like it was going to beat out of my chest. Anxiety would try to take its toll on me as the accuser (Satan) began his harsh mocking, telling me I was unable to articulate words properly, reminding me I spoke Texan, and magnifying my Texas accent in my ears.

Talking in front of people became a giant in my promise land. How could I be a spokeswoman for God when I would almost faint when I was called on to speak? If I received an invitation to be a guest speaker at an event, I would make some kind of lame excuse why I would not be able to accept the invitation. I often encouraged them to seek someone else, giving them names to consider, when all the time I was aching inside wanting to accept the invitation. I am confident in most aspects of ministry, but public speaking is not my forte.

For several years, I served on staff as the Dean of Women at Christ For The Nations Institute in Dallas, Texas. Daily, situations would arise that would present a stretching situation for me. During my tenure there, I was honored to sit on the planning committee for their annual Ladies Conference. We discussed speakers, themes, and anything to do with the event. That was my passion, I loved it.

Time management was very important. The first thing I did each morning when I arrived at my office was check my emails and my mailbox for personal memos. One morning, I noticed a memo from the Director of Women's Ministries. Thinking it concerned updates for the upcoming fall conference, I started to read. For sure, there was an update. To my surprise the memo informed me I was to be one of the breakout speakers for the upcoming conference. Immediately, the taunting began and a feeling of anxiety tried to grip me.

I pondered if I should talk to the director and ask to be released from the assignment or face my giant. Everything within me wanted to accept the invitation. With all the feelings of inadequacy and the voice of the enemy (Satan) mocking me, it was hard to comprehend functioning as the speaker of anything. When you're going through something tough, isn't it difficult to have and hold a steady, objective mind? It is for me. For weeks I grappled with my feelings. Finally, I decided to talk with my assistant and a few of my senior residential assistants. They didn't empathize with me at all. To the contrary, they were excited that I would have the opportunity. They gave me the encouragement I needed to face my insecurities and conquer my giant.

By now, I am sure you're wondering what all this has to do with the word *manifesto*. It has everything to do with it. It was during this time I learned to write and rely on a personal manifesto to stay focused. I wrote down my intentions based on scripture promises. I read and declared my manifesto every day, keeping it ever before me. It helped to keep my mind focused, reminding me of my priorities and who I am in Christ. Let me caution you here, it doesn't matter who says it or how good something sounds, if it can't be substantiated in God's Word, don't go there. The Book of Habakkuk provides evidence that writing a manifesto is validated in God's Word. I like the Message Bible translation of this scripture:

> God answered: Write this. Write what you see. Write it out in big block letters so that it can be read on the run. This vision-message (manifesto) is a witness pointing to what's coming. It aches for the coming—it can hardly wait! And it doesn't lie. If it seems slow in coming, wait. It's on its way. It will come right on time.
>
> Habakkuk 2:2-3, (emphasis mine)

The Word of God is the most powerful manifesto ever written. When we write what God has to say about our individual self or our family, they are not just sweet pretty words. They are words that are alive and powerful (Hebrews 4:11 AMP) and are able to accomplish that for which they are sent. Writing your manifesto based on God's Word will give you the courage to do something about your feelings or situation. I am living proof of the life-changing power in the Word of God. I spoke at the conference and enjoyed every minute. I say the following only to give God the glory and hopefully bring you the needed encouragement to face the giants in your life. When the evaluation sheets of the conference were read, my session assessments were positive and received high kudos. Thank you, Jesus.

Do I still face those feelings of inadequacy? Do I have to deal with those feelings when asked to speak? Most definitely. I'm not naïve enough to believe those old struggles will not try to resurface and that new struggles will not come. When those rough times hit again, I know exactly how to respond because I have already made that decision and commitment to change.

I love going to minister in a church in Midwest City, Oklahoma, because I always leave invigorated by the Holy Spirit. Their worship team ministers with a powerful anointing. I love it when they do this rap son:

> You're somewhere in the future
> and you look much better than
> you look right now. [1]

When I am in a struggle in my spirit, soul or body, I start rapping that song. It's my declaration, calling things that are not as though they were (Romans 4:17 KJV).

How to write a manifesto

There is really no right or wrong way to write a manifesto. The style and intensity of it is up to you.

Your manifesto isn't so much for you to show people. However, if you want to you can, that's your prerogative. A personal manifesto is more of a means, through faith, to see past your present situation into its future outcome. I know that sounds strange, but think about it: Romans 4:17 is a perfect example of believing in a God who can give life to the dead and cause things that do not exist to be as though they do. The Message Bible makes this passage of scriptures clear:

> We call Abraham "father" not because he got God's attention by living like a saint, but because **God made something out of Abraham when he was a nobody.** Isn't that what we've always read in Scripture, God saying to Abraham, "I set you up as father of many peoples."
>
> Abraham was **first named "father"** and **then became a father** because he dared to trust God to do what only God could do: raise the dead to life, with a word make something out of nothing.
>
> When everything was hopeless, Abraham believed anyway, deciding to live not on the basis of what he saw he couldn't do **but on what God said he would do.** And so he was made father of a multitude of peoples. God himself said to him, "You're going to have a big family, Abraham!"
>
> Romans 4:17, (emphasis mine)

I can say with certainty, when I wrote my manifesto based on God's promises, and begin reading it every day, my life was impacted significantly. It helped to focus my attention on what the Word says I am and not what my emotions tell me I am.

Here are a few of my suggestions for writing your personal manifesto:

Choose a topic

You first need to figure out the subject matter you want to write about. For instance, these are the areas in your life which need to be dealt with. I started off with three: Who am I? What does the Word say about who I am? How do I view myself as a public speaker? Write down your beliefs, motives, and intentions about each of the topics you chose.

A personal manifesto is an opportunity for you to lay everything out so you can easily see what you are dealing with. I didn't realize some of the feelings I had about myself until I wrote them down. I dealt with both the pros and the cons of my life. To be honest with you, it was much easier to list my cons rather than my pros. Don't hesitate to write down the positive side of your personality. God made you perfect, and we need to thank Him for the strengths and abilities He put inside us.

When writing your manifesto, you need to use strong, affirmative language:

- Don't use passive phrases like **"I WANT"** to be an Anointed Woman of God.
- Use the more powerful, active phrase like **"I AM"** an Anointed Woman of God. *This may seem elementary to you, but if you use more active language, you will take it more seriously.*

I personally like to use the present tense to make my declaration more powerful: **"I AM _____ ", "MY FAMILY IS _____."**

When I was going through the storm regarding speaking at the Ladies Conference, I daily declared the scriptures used in my manifesto. I declared them in the first person, present tense.

The Lord, the Eternal, equipped me (Nancy) for this job
— with skilled speech, a smooth tongue for instruction.
Isaiah 50:4, Voice Bible, (emphasis mine)
The Spirit of the Lord is upon **Nancy**, because the Lord
has anointed and commissioned me **Nancy** to _____.
Isaiah 61:1, AMP, (emphasis mine)

Use pen and paper

You should consider writing your manifesto with pen and paper.
When you physically write something using an actual pen and
paper, it seems to generate more power symbolically. I know we
are in an age of technology, and it is true, we need to be tech
savvy in order to better communicate. However, there is
something about taking time and actually writing something on
paper that will, at the same time, cause the subject to be
imprinted into your mind. That's one way of renewing your mind
as we are told to do in the Word.

In Conclusion

Praying Mama, I am not sure where your confidence level is.
However, I can assure you, God is raising up individuals in this
hour to make changes in our culture. These changes will affect
our families, churches, cities, regions, and nations. Yes, you are
one of those people!

Be assured, God had you, your sons and daughters in
mind when He made known His manifesto regarding the last day
move of the Spirit. He made known His intent publicly regarding
Praying Mamas and their children when He inspired the Prophet
Joel to write:

I am going to pour out my Spirit on every kind of people,
and He said, Your sons and daughters will prophesy.
Joel 2:28

That is an imperative statement concerning His manifesto,
regarding Praying Mamas and their children.

We have entered into a new era. Many are calling it an Era of Conquest. According to the Merriam Webster's Collegiate Dictionary, the definition of *conquest* is "to overcome and take control of (a place or people) by use of military force."

It excited me when I thought of what Holy Spirit said about Praying Mamas. "These Powerful Mamas are a force to be reckoned with. They are my End-Time Heroes!"

I hope this gives you a better understanding of the word *manifesto* and why I was prompted to use it in conjunction with "Praying Mamas."

It is my prayer that you will be inspired not only to write your values down, but to create an entire manifesto for your life and the life of your family.

Not only will it grow you as a Praying Mama, but it will help you live out those beliefs. And, when all is said and done, a distinctive feature of being a Woman of Valor, a Praying Mama, **"Is knowing what you believe, and having the grace to live it."**

Psalm 91

COVENANT PRAYER FOR PRAYING MAMAS

This Covenant Prayer is to be prayed over yourself or your beloved tribe. **PAUSE, PONDER AND PRAY**. It is God's Shield of Protection for your children and whosoever will. Copy and enlarge it — inserting his/her name in the blanks.

_____ dwells in the shelter of the Most High and he/she abides in the shadow of the Almighty. _____ says to the Lord, "My refuge and my fortress, my God, in whom I trust!"

For it is God who delivers _____ from the snare of the trapper and from the deadly pestilence (fatal, infectious disease.) God will cover _____ with His pinions, and under His wings _____ may seek refuge: God's faithfulness is a shield and bulwark.

_____ will not be afraid of the terror by night, or of the arrow that flies by day; of the pestilence that stalks in darkness, or of the destruction that lays waste at noon. A thousand may fall at _____'s side and 10,000 at his/her right hand, but it shall not approach _____. _____ will only look on with _____'s eyes and see the recompense of the wicked.

For _____ has made the Lord his/her refuge, even the Most High, _____'s dwelling place. No evil will befall _____, nor will any plague come near _____'s tent. For He will give His angels charge concerning _____ to guard _____ in all his/her ways. They will bear _____ up in their hands, lest _____ strike his/her foot against a stone. _____ will tread upon the lion and cobra, the young lion and the serpent he/she will trample down.

Because _____ has loved Me (God said), therefore I will deliver him/her; I will set _____ securely on high, because _____ has known My Name. _____ will call on Me, and I will answer _____. I will be with _____ in trouble; I will rescue _____ and honor _____. With a long life I will satisfy _____, and let him/her behold My salvation."

First Things First

Praying Mama, Hannah
No doubt, Hannah wept when she left her first born at the House of God. However, since she had made a vow to God concerning her son, she kept her promise. As a result, God rewarded her with more children. Her first-born son, Samuel, faithfully served God his entire life and became one of the most beloved rulers in Israel.

— Mother of the Prophet Samuel

> The Lord gives the command;The women who proclaim the good news are a great host (army).
> Psalm 68:11, AMP

Praying Mamas, let's not get the cart before the horse. We are in a Civil War; this war is between God and Satan, good vs. evil. All we need to do is listen to the news or read newspaper headlines to perceive the focus of this war is, without a doubt, for our families and future generations.

Satan is a remorseless thief and killer, and he is after our children. Here are only two recent headlines that I have in my chronicles of news segments: **Killing The Next Generation.**

- May 23, 2017, headlines in the *New York Post:* **Killing Our Kids.** At least 19 dead.

- November 8, 2017, headlines of the *Chicago Tribune* concerning the Texas church shooting: **Death sweeps across 3 generations of a single family gathered at church.** In all, eight members of their family are dead. *Please note: This shooting took place just a few miles from our home.*

Jesus taught his disciples about this killer:

> The thief's purpose is to steal and KILL and destroy. My purpose is to give them a rich and satisfying life.
>
> John 10:6, PTP

If you study the Greek word for *kill*, the word *thuo* is used. It is not the word for *kill*. It is defined as "sacrifice or slaughter." The word *kill* is not the lesser of these two evils; the results and the pain are synonymous. However, "sacrifice or slaughter" is a stronger appellation of the word *kill*. The word *slaughter* imprints an indelible picture in our minds which will not be easily forgotten. The chief killer is Satan himself. He is busy slaughtering unborn babies and sacrificing children, even while you are reading this text. According to ask.com, every year in the world there are an estimated 40-50 million abortions. This corresponds to approximately 125,000 abortions per day.

> In the USA, where nearly half of pregnancies are unintended and four in ten of these are terminated by abortion, there are over 3,000 abortions per day. Twenty-two percent of all pregnancies in the USA (excluding miscarriages) end in abortion.[1]

Mamas, I address you singularly. Like Esther in the Bible, perhaps you were placed in the Kingdom for such a time as this; however, only **You** can make the commitment to save yourself and future generations from complete annihilation.

When we are on a spiritual high, it is easy to say, "If I die, I die." Realistically, it is hard to put into practice when opposition occurs. God has given you His authority and ability to stop these horrendous acts of injustice. You alone can make

---

[1] **http://www.worldometers.info/abortions**, accessed February 22, 2019.

the decision to do so. You need to stop and ponder this statement Bobby Conner said concerning the power of personal intercession:

> I was shown that one individual on their knees, connected to God in prayer, is more powerful than all the armies of the world. Can you imagine it? One little frail grandmother on her knees before the Throne of Almighty God, generates more power and effects more than all the world powers armies.[1]

God spent a lot of time in the Bible telling us who we are and who we are destined to be. Equally true, in relentless pursuit, Satan's main goal is to make us doubt who we are and who God destined us to be.

There is an identity crisis going on in both the natural and spiritual world in which we live. On a daily basis we are warned about identity theft and instructed how not to fall victim of the thieves who want to compromise our family's identities.

> Every two seconds, another American becomes a victim of identity fraud. The number of identity fraud victims jumped to 13.1 million in 2013, a new report from Javelin Strategy & Research finds. That's an increase of 500,000 from 2012 and the second highest number of victims since Javelin began conducting its annual study in 2004.[2]

The first glimpse of Satan and his cunning schemes was in the garden. If you read the complete narrative in Genesis Chapter 3, the first case of identity theft is evident, and it involved the very

---

[1] The Courts and Council of God, *The Shepherd's Rod*, 2017.
[2] Blake Ellis, *Identity fraud hits new victim every two seconds*, money.cnn.com, February 6, 2014.

first mother, Eve. The battle over our Divine destinies and identities has never ceased. It has only intensified. Revelation 12:13-17 speaks of the intensity of this war:

> When the dragon realized he had been cast down to the earth, he pursued the mother of the male infant. In order to escape the serpent, she was given the two wings of the great eagle to fly deeper into the wilderness to her own special place where she would find sustenance for a time, and times, and half a time. Then from his mouth the serpent spewed water like a raging river that chased after the woman, trying to sweep her away in the flood. But the earth came to her rescue. It opened its gaping mouth and swallowed the river that spewed from the dragon's mouth. As a result, the dragon was enraged at the woman and went away to make war on the rest of her children.
>
> The Voice Bible

The first war involved the very first mother. The end-time war involves an army of Kingdom-minded mothers united with a passion and single-mindedness (Psalm 68:11).

> The Lord gives the word; and many women are ready to tell the good news.

The Hebrew translation of the word *basara* is: messenger, preach, publish, shew forth, (bear, bring, carry, preach, good, tell good) tidings.[1] I will render my own translation of this scripture.

> The Lord gives the word. Many Praying Mamas are ready to show forth the good news and declare war for the impending generations.

---

[1] Psalm 68.
https://biblehub.com/commentaries/barnes/psalms/68.htm.

It will not be just one voice who declares God's Word. It is a concerted effort of an army of many united voices. These Spirit-filled Praying Mamas engage in the conflict over the identities and Divine destinies of this millennial generation, the prime target of the dragon himself.

Before proceeding any further, we need to establish these facts. If you have not given birth to biological children, you are not exempt from this war. You are a mother to someone, it's in your DNA. You have spiritual sons and daughters who need to be rescued from the camp of the enemy. *Grandmas, your age is no excuse, you are called to battle, and the younger generation needs your wisdom.* If you are reading this book, it is time to arise and advance. We need to rise in the area of authority and move in the Power of Holy Spirit living within us.

As end-time warriors, we must be cognizant of the fact that we are in a real war, *good vs. evil.* More importantly, we need to face the reality that in order to successfully win this war, we must have a full understanding of the following:1) WE MUST KNOW OUR GOD, 2) WE MUST KNOW OUR ENEMY and 3)WE MUST KNOW OURSELVES.

The Art of War, by Sun Tzu, is one of the greatest books on the subject of war ever written. Focusing on ancient Chinese military strategies and tactics, the philosophies became important strategies in warfare. Sun Tzu is quoted as saying:

> It is said that if you know your enemies and know yourself, you will not be put at risk even in a hundred battles.[1]

I like to research historical wars. I believe natural wars and spiritual wars run parallel with each other in their functionality. If you study military strategies, you soon perceive that an army must know their enemy in order to defeat him in battle. It is not enough to simply recognize Satan's existence or to be conscious

---

[1] Sun Tzu; https://www.brainyquote.com/authors/sun_tzu.

of his presence on Earth. It is imperative that we become acutely aware of his strategies. To the degree we are ignorant of his schemes, to that degree he takes advantage of us. In his instructions to the Corinthians Paul said:

> It's my duty to make sure that Satan does not win even a small victory over us, for we don't want to be naïve and then fall prey to his schemes.
> 2 Corinthians 2:11, The Voice Bible

General Sun Tzu also maintains in his strategies of war that not only should you know your enemy well, but you must also know yourself. Praying Mamas, when engaging in spiritual warfare, there are true military actions that you must understand, but first and foremost, you must **Know Your God**. If you don't know God and what He has to say in His Word about spiritual wars, it is futile to engage in a war you cannot win.

This book is about you and the battles you are presently engaged in, and the battles you will face in the future! God has included you in His end-time manifesto. His list of intentions is written throughout the Bible. His purpose for you and your family is stunning. If you read nothing more than the first few chapters of this book, my hopes are that you will fully comprehend who you are in Christ and know your God more intimately than ever before. You have what it takes to engage in the battle for the generations to come.

Praying Mamas, I ask you this question, *If we don't, who will?* We are the catalysts for change. I believe God has given us an opportunity to be a part of one of the greatest prayer movements the world has ever seen. Mothers around the world, with one purpose in mind, are going to shift their families, which will in turn shift our schools, cities, regions and the nations of the world.

NOTE: As a result of a Praying Mama, Hannah, Samuel faithfully served God and the nation of Israel as it transitioned from the time of judges to the rule of kings.

Young Samuel was placed under the care and training of Eli, the priest and judge of Israel at that time He also served as a teacher and prophet.

Toward the end of the period of the judges of Israel, the roughly 300 years between Joshua and King Saul, God began preparing a child who would have profound leadership skills and spiritual steadfastness to judge Israel. After Samuel began serving as judge, he continued in this role "all the days of his life" (1 Samuel 7:15).

The Amplified Bible translates *Selah* as "pause, and think of that." It can also be interpreted as a form of underlining in preparation for the next paragraph. Another interpretation claims that *Selah* comes from the primary Hebrew root word *Selah* (סָלָה), which means "to hang" and by implication "to measure (weigh)".[1]

I will conclude each chapter with a *Selah*, suggesting you take a moment to **PAUSE–PONDER–PRAY.**

---

[1] Selah - Wikipedia https://en.wikipedia.org/wiki/Selah.

סֶלָה

SELAH
PAUSE–PONDER–PRAY

PAUSE
If you want to change the world... start off by making your bed.

Admiral William H. McRaven, U. S. Navy, retired, said this about his Navy Seal training:

> "Throughout my life in the Navy, making my bed was the one constant that I could count on every day." Making my bed correctly was not going to be an opportunity for praise. It was expected of me. It was my first task of the day, and doing it right was important. It demonstrated my discipline. It showed my attention to detail, and at the end of the day it would be a reminder that I had done something well, something to be proud of, no matter how small the task.[1]

PONDER
As mothers, sometimes we don't feel like World Changers. Most of the time we feel like we don't even change diapers well. Previously, I shared Philippians 4:13 with you. Take a Selah

---

[1] University of Texas at Austin 2014 Commencement Address - Admiral William H. McRaven, **https://www.youtube.com/watch?v=pxBQLFLei70**, May 14, 2014.

moment to reflect on it. Declare it in the first person, until the perspective of yourself begins to change. If you need to write a Personal Manifesto, do so.

> I can do all things [which He has called me to do] through Him who strengthens and empowers me [to fulfill His purpose — I am self-sufficient in Christ's sufficiency; I am ready for anything and equal to anything through Him who infuses me with inner strength and confident peace.]
>
> Philippians 4:13, AMP

PRAY

Heavenly Father, I realize I can do nothing within my own strength and ability. If I am to be part of your End-time Manifesto and do what You have asked me to do, you will have to strengthen me by Your Holy Spirit. Right now, I open my heart and ask you to fill me with the power of the Holy Spirit in order to fulfill what You have told me to do!

I pray this in Jesus' Name. Amen!

CHAPTER 2

Know Your God

Praying Mama: Sonya Carson

Sonya Carson put her total self into making sure her sons did their best in school. Oftentimes, she worked long hours and two to three jobs to keep the Carson family afloat.

Her relationship and dependence on the Lord provided her with the wisdom to raise her boys to graduate from high school, college, and become successful men. She did this while living as a single mom in the inner cities of Boston and Detroit. Sonya Carson's life motto is:

"Learn to do your best and God will do the rest."

— Mother of Dr. Ben Carson

People who know their God shall prove themselves strong and shall stand firm and do exploits [for God].

Daniel 11:32, AMP

In my preteen and teen years, I was privileged to meet and enjoy the ministry of several great revivalists. Oral Roberts, the great healing evangelist in the 1948 revival, was almost an icon to me. I was young and couldn't fully comprehend what happened when he walked into the room. I just knew when he entered, something electrifying seemed to happen. I now understand it was The Presence of Jesus, which seemed almost tangible.

Born in a Christian home, I was taught about God at an early age. I loved Him and had a knowledge of Him, but I really couldn't enjoy Him. Like many others in those days, my perception of Him was, *He's a God of punishment and vengeance, just waiting for me to make a mistake so He could pour out His wrath upon me.* Even though I loved Him, to a degree I was afraid of Him. A head-knowledge of God, without a relationship with Him, is a miserable way to live.

In the early years of Oral Robert's ministry, his theme song was *God Is A Good God.* That song touched the lives of many, including myself, changing their preconceived idea of Father God. The lyrics went like this:

God is a good God!
Every heartache, He understands.
There is healing power, there are miracles
in the touch of His Wonderful Hands.

What He's done for others
He will do for you,
If you'll only believe and trust Him too.
For God is a good God, and
His goodness He will show to you.[1]

Singing those lyrics week after week released into Earth's atmosphere the truth about God, changing the lives of thousands of people. If your knowledge of God has been tainted by some erroneous teachings of man, you need to pause and meditate on the lyrics of that song and what the written Word has to say about Him.

God is a good God! He loves you so much He gave His only Son for the redemption of you, your household and the entire world. The Message Bible says it like this:

---

[1] *God is a good God,*
https://www.youtube.com/watch?v=Hc89G_kf9e8. Written/sung by Stuart Hamblen. Music arranged and conducted by Ralph Carmichael 1956.

This is how much God loved the world: He gave his Son, his one and only Son. And this is why: so that no one need be destroyed; by believing in him, anyone can have a whole and lasting life. God didn't go to all the trouble of sending his Son merely to point an accusing finger, telling the world how bad it was. He came to help, to put the world right again. Anyone who trusts in him is acquitted; anyone who refuses to trust him has long since been under the death sentence without knowing it. And why? Because of that person's failure to believe in the one-of-a-kind Son of God when introduced to him.

John 3:16-18, MSG

While writing this section of Know Your God, Holy Spirit impressed upon me that many of you feel as if both you and your family have been sabotaged by the enemy with little hope of liberation from his oppressive hold. Again, I remind you, God is a one-of-a-kind God and He is Good:

The Lord is good, A strength and stronghold in the day of trouble; He knows [He recognizes, cares for, and understands fully] those who take refuge and trust in Him.

Nahum 1:7, AMP

The Voice Bible narrative of the account of Paul and Silas brings a message of assurance to those who feel imprisoned without any hope of liberation:

Jailer: "Gentlemen, please tell me, what must I do to be liberated?"
Paul and Silas: "Just believe, believe in the ultimate (one-of-a-kind) King Jesus, and not only

will you be rescued, but your whole household as well."

Acts 16:29-30, (paraphrase mine)

We serve a mighty God, and there is nothing too hard for Him. There are no circumstances you and I face that God cannot handle. It doesn't make Him nervous when we mess up and need to start over. With God, it is never too late for restoration.

In those early crusades I witnessed first-hand God's healing power and the following phrase was on everybody's lips, "Move over, devil; I'm coming through." Those words became the motto of our household even after my husband and I married and had children of our own.

Not only did I learn about the goodness of God, I also learned we have been given His authority to tell the devil to move out of the way. *I don't have the time to mess with you today, or any other day as far as that goes.* Recently, our little six-year-old great-granddaughter, Sayla, was doing a Facebook-live video. Her comment about the devil was a classic. She said, "The devil is rude, and we don't like him, so don't listen to him."

In this new era, in which we are a part, for those who seek Him, the Holy Spirit is going to restore the reverential fear of the Lord, and an intimate knowledge of who He really is. There is no substitute for intimacy for those who truly want to know Him.

When you get to know God, great things begin to happen in your life and in the lives of your family. You become fully aware of the fact that daily He fights for you and your family. He is not against you; He is for you. Notice I said, "Daily, God fights for you and your family." The question is, "Are you fighting with Him?"

Mamas, we are not alone in the battle for our family, God is partnering with us. He would never let us go to war single-handedly. Yes, you are a mighty warrior but again I reiterate, it is imperative that you know the character of God. He is a loving Father with a heart for the restoration of all things, especially our families.

My husband and I are in our 58th year of marriage. Our mantra was, and still is, Romans 8:31. "If God be for us, who could be against us." The Passion Bible says it so well:

> So what does all this mean? If God has determined to stand with us, tell me, who then could ever stand against us? For God has proven His love by giving us His greatest treasure, the gift of His Son. And since God freely offered Him up as the sacrifice for us all, He certainly won't withhold from us anything else He has to give. Who would dare to accuse those whom God has chosen in love to be His own.
>
> Romans 8:31, TPT, paraphrase

I believe it saddened God to say, "My people are destroyed because of a lack of knowledge of Me" (Hosea 4:4, paraphrase mine). I like the Message Bible's account of that verse, "My people are ruined because they don't know what's right or true."

I declare, in this new era, we will not be ruined, "We will know our God," and what is right and true.

It's disturbing to me when I hear well-meaning teachers and counselors tell those who have suffered great loss, "It's okay to be mad at God." Our pastor friend and spiritual son, who is currently grieving the sudden death of his 57-year-old father, relayed the following story to me. He said when he was in his teens, one of his teachers told him, "It's okay to be mad at God." He said, "This brought some confusion to me because it contradicted what my father taught me." Upon returning home from school that day, he told his dad what his teacher said to him and wanted to know if it was correct. His father's response speaks volumes:

> "Your teacher had no idea what she was talking about.
> Being mad at God would be like being mad at money
when you're broke.

Being mad at God would be like being mad at God when you're hungry. Being mad at God would be like being mad at water when you're dehydrated."

He concluded with this, "Don't do it again." Even though there are questions as to why his father was taken at such a crucial time in his life, he in turn asked me the following question, "Why would people want to be mad at God? He didn't cause it; He is our only hope."[1]

You may be puzzled how to familiarize yourself with God and rightly respect Him. You are not alone in the quest of getting to know God. The Bible gives us clear, precise instructions how to get acquainted with God. The Holy Spirit is our Teacher, and we are to ask Him to teach us to fear and revere the Lord so we can, in turn, correctly instruct the upcoming generations:

> *Come, you children, listen to me;* I will teach you to fear the Lord (with awe-inspire reverence and worship Him with obedience).
> Psalm 34:11, AMP

I like the way Job said it. He had suffered great loss. However, he put it in the right perspective when he told his friends, who were bringing accusations against God:

> Acquaint now thyself with him, and be at peace: thereby good shall come unto thee. If thou return to the Almighty, thou shalt be built up, thou shalt put away iniquity far from thy tabernacles. Then shalt thou lay up gold as dust, and the gold of Ophir as the stones of the brooks. Yea, the Almighty shall be thy defense,

---

[1] Isaac Tucker, Pastor of the New Harvest Life International Church, Midwest City, Oklahoma.

and thou shalt have plenty of silver. For then shalt thou have thy delight in the Almighty, and shalt lift up thy face unto God. Thou shalt make thy prayer unto him, and he shall hear thee, and thou shalt pay thy vows. Thou shalt also decree a thing, and it shall be established unto thee: and the light shall shine upon thy ways.

Job 22:21, 23-28, KJV, (emphasis mine)

Our heart's cry should be:
"Lord I want to know You."
"Praise the LORD! Hallelujah!"

Blessed [fortunate, prosperous, and favored by God] is the man/woman who fears the LORD [with awe-inspired reverence and worships Him with obedience], Who delights greatly in His commandments. His descendants will be mighty on the earth; The generation of the upright will be blessed.

Psalm 112:1-2, AMP (paraphrase mine)

That's good news! Isn't it a comfort to know God has given us His Holy Spirit to individually teach us, lead and guide us in mothering and warring for our unique children, the Millennial Generation?

True, we are in a war, but the war has already been won through Christ's accomplishment on the cross. Sun Tzu, the Chinese General said:

"Every battle is won BEFORE it is fought."[1]

---

[1] Sun Tzu; **https://www.brainyquote.com/authors/sun_tzu**. Accessed February 24, 2019.

Sun Tzu had no idea he was prophesying what Jesus accomplished on the cross. When Jesus made his final declaration, He made it known to all, both in Heaven and on Earth.

> I have accomplished and fulfilled all my Father
> sent me to do and "**It Is Finished!**"
>
> John 19:30, KJV

Praying Mamas, the enemy is an intimidator, and he tries to threaten his rivals in order to get them to do what he wants. When the enemy gets in your face (trust me he will) bringing accusations against you and your descendants, with confidence you can rest in the fact that he has been defeated. *Your battles have been won, even before they start. Jesus has already won them for you.* With boldness you can declare Jesus' own words, "It Is Finished" or "It Is Written."

"It Is Finished" and "It Is Written" should be in your pantry of warfare staples. When the enemy hears those words, they strike fear in his heart and the hearts of his cohorts as well. Jesus' declaration "It Is Finished" made public the enemy's demise. "It Is Written" are the words Jesus decreed when He was in war with the devil over His Divine destiny and identity.

It saddens me to read the account of the crucifixion, but it excites me to no end when I read the last words of Jesus. He gave a mandate to the disciple John to take care of His mother. He said, "Look after and provide for her." That definitive statement was declared, not just for His mother alone, but for all mothers of future generations. What a prophetic picture of God's intent for the Praying Mamas who are mentioned in His end-time manifesto. "Look after and provide for her." You, Praying Mama, are the one He is talking about. Take heart, you are not in the battle alone.

Mothers, there is nothing about you that Satan likes. He knows God has anointed you and has made sure you have everything you need spirit, soul and body to reach your Divine destiny. God has marked you as His end-time warriors and that is the core reason the opposer, Satan, is coming against you and your family so hard. His greatest fear is Spirit-filled women who have a passion to take back what rightfully belongs to God: our children. The devil dreads the sight and sound of a mother who knows her authority in Christ. Praying Mamas, you are *the ones God has been waiting for.*

Let me conclude with these statements about God.

Our God Is Omniscient.
This means He is all knowing. He sees all and knows all. He knows everything about us, every word we say before we say it, every thought before we think it. He knows the end from the beginning of our lives. Guess what? In spite of all our mess-ups, He still loves us more than we can comprehend. The enemy doesn't want you to know this about God. He would rather you think God is out to get you because of your past, but that is far from the truth. He loves us in spite of our weaknesses. In the Psalms, the psalmist David wrote this about his God:

> How great is our God! There's absolutely nothing his power cannot accomplish, and he has infinite understanding of everything.
> Psalm 147:5, TPT

> Lord, you know everything there is to know about me. You perceive every movement of my heart and soul, and you understand my every thought before it even enters my mind. You are so intimately aware of me, Lord. You read my heart like an open book and you know all the words I'm about to speak before I even start a sentence! You know every step I take, even before my journey begins. You've gone into my future to prepare the way, and in kindness you follow behind me to spare me from the harm of my past. With your hand of love upon me you impart a blessing to me. This is just too

wonderful, deep and incomprehensible! Your understanding of me brings me wonder and strength.

Psalm 139:1-6, TPT

God Is Omnipresent.
He can be everywhere at the same time. He never sleeps nor slumbers. Every moment of every day He knows exactly what we're up against and is with us always.

> He will not let your foot slip — he who watches over you will not slumber.
>
> Psalm 121:3, AMPC

> The eyes of the Lord are in every place, keeping watch on the evil and the good.
>
> Proverbs 15:3, AMPC

God Is Omnipotent.
I enjoy the word potent when talking about God. It gives us a clear picture of how powerful He really is. Omnipotent means He has great power, great influence and great effect. He is all powerful. He reigns supreme. He strengthens us. His Holy Spirit guides us and empowers us. His Word reminds us that He fights for us. He alone holds the power to forgive, the power to set free, the power to save, and the power to give eternal life. God is a potent symbol of authority.

> For nothing will be impossible with God.
>
> Luke 1:37, NKJV

The Voice Bible says it like this:
"The impossible is possible with God."
It is never too late for the impossibles in the lives of our families to be possible. You can rest assured that God is with you in the present battle you are engaged in, and He has the final say about the outcome of the battle!

He can do ANYTHING. Isn't that just freeing to know that you don't have to rely on your own strength or circumstances? If you're in a season of waiting, if you're in a place where you feel like giving up, "Press on; hold on." Your time is coming. He will come to you with an even greater plan than you have for yourself.

Just keep moving, believing and praying. And knowing down to your very bones, He can do anything, even when it doesn't look like it in the natural. Believing, even when our circumstances say it differently than what my Father has said, …*That's faith!* The One who names every star and created the heavens with a WORD is looking out for you. In the Book of Luke, chapter 12, it even says:

> Since you are so much more precious to God than a thousand flocks of sparrows, and since God knows you in every detail—down to the number of hairs on your head at this moment— you can be secure and unafraid of any person, and you have nothing to fear from God either.

I mean, He knows the very number of hairs on your head. Think about that. Take a deep breath of peace today knowing that He has you in the palm of His hand.[1]

Praying Mamas, we must know who God is in order for us to know who He has destined us to become. Let me remind you of this Truth:

> The fear of the Lord leads to life: Then one rests content, untouched by Trouble.
>
> Proverbs 19:23, NIV

The teacher sums it all up in his concluding statement as he reminds the reader to remember his Creator:

---

[1] Jessica Hart; Facebook Post 5-6-18.

My advice to you is to remember your Creator,
God.

Ecclesiastes 12:1, The Voice Bible

Praying Mamas, it would behoove you when in the heat of the
battle, take time to remember and praise God for who He is and
the victories He has already won on your behalf. Don't let the
battle become bigger than the God you serve. Never forget:

> Greater is He who is in you, than He who is in
> the world.

1 John 4:4, KJV

סֶ֫לָה

SELAH
PAUSE–PONDER–PRAY

PAUSE

When you get to know God, great things will begin to happen in your life and in the lives of your family.

PONDER
The great Reformation hymn, *A Mighty Fortress Is Our God,*[1] gives revelation as to why we need to Know Our God.

> A mighty fortress is our God, A Bulwark never failing; Our Helper He, amid the flood Of mortal ills prevailing: For still our ancient foe Doth seek to work us woe; His craft and pow'r are great, And, armed with cruel hate, On earth is not his equal.
>
> Did we in our own strength confide, Our striving would be losing; Were not the right Man on our side, The Man of God's own choosing: Dost ask who that may be? Christ Jesus, it is He; Lord Sabaoth His Name, From age to age the same, And He must win the battle.
>
> And though this world, with devils filled, Should threaten to undo us, We will not fear, for God hath willed His truth to triumph through us:

---

[1] Martin Luther, *A Mighty Fortress Is Our God*, https://en.wikipedia.org/wiki/A_Mighty_Fortress_Is_Our_God.

The Prince of Darkness grim, We tremble not for him; His rage we can endure, For lo! his doom is sure, One little word shall fell him.

That word above all earthly pow'rs, No thanks to them, abideth; The Spirit and the gifts are ours Through Him Who with us sideth: Let goods and kindred go, This mortal life also; The body they may kill: God's truth abideth still, His kingdom is forever.

PRAY

Father, I thank you that you are a Mighty Fortress for those who are weary from all the problems, hassles and challenges that have come against them. Many may think that I am strong, but I know my strength and fortitude is due to your faithfulness to me. Thank you for hiding me in the cleft of the rock and continuing to strengthen me until I bring this assignment to a victorious end! I pray this in Jesus' Name. Amen!

CHAPTER 3

Know Yourself

Praying Mama: Mary Ball Washington

Known as The Bulletproof President, George Washington was the first president of the United States. Before he left for war, it is said that he knelt before his mother's rocking chair while she prayed for God's protection on his life. Washington later credited his mother's prayers for his surviving many crises and several massacres in the British campaigns that followed.

George said "By the all-powerful dispensation of Providence, I have been protected beyond all human probability or expectation; for I had four bullets through my coat, and two horses shot under me, yet escaped unhurt, although death was leveling my companions on every side of me!"

— Mother of George Washington

> For we are God's masterpiece. He has created us anew in Christ Jesus, so we can do the good things he planned for us long ago.
>
> Ephesians 2:10, NLT

Have you ever entertained these questions? *Why am I here on planet Earth? What is my purpose? Where do I fit? Who am I?* If your answer is "Yes," you can rest assured you are not alone. This litany of questions has haunted every human being born on the face of Earth. We all have an innate desire to know our true identity and purpose in life. Identity crisis is real and not just a catchphrase in our culture.

In his book, *In Pursuit of Purpose*, the late Myles Munroe wrote this statement:

"It is dangerous to be alive and not know why you were given life."[1]

I was privileged to be born into a family of ministers. My great-grandfather was ordained with the Assemblies of God in 1914 and pastored the first Apostolic church in the Austin area until his untimely death at the age of 36. I am a fourth-generation wife of a pastor.

Born in a pastor's home, I was schooled at an early age on how to conduct myself. I was the first born of the clan and the package included a strong-willed little girl with a motor mouth. I was a tomboy and one might say my five older uncles didn't help matters. They only made things worse. My mother was challenged with the tough job of trying to train me to be a young lady. Often times she would tell me, "Little girls are to be seen and not heard." That statement still tries to govern my life, and I am 78 years old. Words we speak over our children can produce a negative influence in their personality development.

A little humor here, two things were instilled in me by my grandparents. My grandmother told me not to use the word "pregnant" when talking about an expectant mother. My grandfather adamantly told me, after I addressed an elder of the church by his first name, "You never address an elder by his first name, always use the preface 'Brother'." Those were serious admonitions, and I needed to take heed of them if I didn't want the wrath of God and my grandparents to come down upon me. I still choke on the word "pregnant", and I would dare not address a minister by his first name!

Soon after I married, my great-grandmother, who was a very proper lady and functioned in the role of a minister's wife herself, requested to talk with me. As the matriarch of the family,

[1] Myles Munroe, In Pursuit Of Purpose, Preface: Destiny Image Publisher Inc.

she advised me how to properly represent my husband in ministry, the dos and don'ts, how to sit, what not to wear. She covered everything I needed to know in order to appropriately function as a minister's wife. Her instructions were honorable, but they began the process of a fake identity in my life. Even though I was privileged to be his wife, that was not the entirety of my destiny. Like many wives of prominent men in ministry or in the secular world, our identities can be easily sabotaged. As for me, I began to wear the name tag "Preacher's Wife," which in turn became my identity. I wore that badge with honor, but it was not the totality of my God-ordained identity. It was the way mankind viewed me.

After a few years of marriage, and several visits to the church her son and I were pastoring, my late mother-in-law decided to attend a ladies' retreat of which I was in charge. Later when we were discussing the event, out of nowhere she suggested that perhaps I should be a little more like a certain pastor's wife whom she highly respected. I had a good relationship with my mother-in-law, and in most cases, respected her opinions. But in this case, the woman she chose to be my role model was not like me in any form or fashion. I tried, but her shoes just didn't fit my feet. You see, combat boots fit me much better than the glass slippers she wore. Again, my individuality was challenged which made an indelible impression on my soul, raising the question, *Who Am I?*

Praying Mamas, I know from experience, wearing a counterfeit tag of identity can make you feel despondent and have hope deferred. If we try to function in life with no idea of our significance and relevance, we begin having moments of discouragement and loss of purpose. Living without the knowledge of who you were destined to be causes you to develop a people-pleasing disorder, and the fear of man becomes a giant in your life. King David, in the Bible, didn't have a soft spot in his heart for giants, and neither should we. Giants are a detriment to our health and identity.

Don't misunderstand me; I am grateful for my rich lineage and all the well-meaning advice given me. I wasn't by any means rebellious. I just could not function as the person everybody wanted me to be. I like the old adage, *Being born in a garage doesn't make you a car.* In my case, being born in a pastor's home certainly did not define my God-given, prophetic destiny.

God, in His sovereignty, uniquely designed each of us for our own purpose, and we are perfect for the task. He didn't make two of a kind; that is amazing to me. My purpose is far greater than sporting glass slippers and sitting on the front seat of the church, wearing my infamous fake smile, in order to make my husband look good. It was impossible to function in the role they put me in. Can you identify with this? Surely, I am not the only one who has experienced the people-pleasing syndrome.

I love and respect all who have spoken into my life, but I could not fulfill all their expectations, because expectations don't always match reality. I tried to achieve all their beliefs of what I should and should not be, but the reality was, the armor they gave me just didn't fit. It was too big and cumbersome for me to use. Misery was my constant companion.

I encourage you to ask the Holy Spirit to help you rise above the expectations of man. Praying Mamas, never compare yourself to anyone. God has uniquely designed you with a definite purpose in mind. Your existence in this particular time in history is evidence that the generations needs something that your life contains. There is no one on the face of Earth like you.

Get to know who you are and who God has ordained you to be. You are a history maker destined to change the world around you. If we want to change the nations of the world, we must change the way we view ourselves and those in our sphere of influence. Pause and meditate on the following statement by Bobby Conner:

> Think about it! You are Divinely unique, no other human on earth is like you! Amid the seven billion plus people alive on this planet God has made only one you. One of the criteria for placing value on an object is how rare is it? You

were chosen by God in eternity past to live in the present, to forge the future.[1]

There is only one of you. You have your own set of fingerprints, DNA and voiceprint[2]; you are one of a kind which makes you unique and valuable. It has been said, "Something is only worth what someone is willing to pay for it." That's how valuable, significant and loved you are. You are worth what Jesus was willing to pay. With His own life, Jesus declared your worth:

> Greater love has no one than this, that someone lay down his life for his friends.
>
> John 15:13, ESV

No wonder the enemy tries so hard to blind you of your worth in the Kingdom. God planned your personality and destiny even before He created the world. He had need of you to fulfill His commitment to restore all things. God strategically placed you in the Kingdom for such a time as this. You are a Kingdom Advancer. It is vital that you discover your purpose in life and go after it relentlessly or you will fail to live a rich, whole, meaningful life.

"You must realize that **your fulfillment in life is dependent on your becoming and doing what you were born to be and do.** Anything less makes life your enemy and death your friend. It is essential, vital, crucial and necessary that you understand this fundamental principle of purpose and pursue it with all your heart. **For without purpose, life has no heart.** Remember,

---

[1] Bobby Conner's book, *Master's Plan Divine Design*; back cover.

[2] **https://www.yourdictionary.com/voiceprint**. Accessed 03/29/2019.

those who don't know where they are going will probably end up somewhere else."[1]

Therefore, I do not run like a man running aimlessly. 1 Corinthians 9:26, (emphasis mine)

God made us in His divine image and has given us a mandate along with His authority to be His representatives on Earth. We are destined to change the lives of future generations who have lost or have no knowledge of their God-given purpose or identity. We are not just warring for our individual identities. We are also in combat for the identity and Divine prophetic destiny of our children and grandchildren.

Mike Foster says it so well in his book, *People of the Second Chance.*

Identity is the engine that drives the relationship not only with ourselves but also with God and others. If your identity is broken, your life is broken. If you define it incorrectly, you will carry that wrong definition into your story. If all you see are your limitations, you will miss out on the stunning possibilities God is creating in front of you.[2]

Satan knows there is power in our identity. He greatly fears the woman who knows her true purpose in life. That is why he fights so hard to keep us from knowing who we really are and why we are here on planet Earth. Like Mike Foster said, "If your identity is broken, your life is broken."

---

[1] Myles Munroe, In Pursuit Of Purpose, Preface: Destiny Image Publisher Inc.

[2] Mike Foster; *People of the Second Chance: A Guide to Bringing Life-saving Love to the World.* CO Springs, CO: WaterBrook, 2016. p. 8-9.

It shouldn't be a surprise that the first battle began in the garden. His plan was, and still is, to rob us of the very substance of our life, our identity. It was at the center of the garden, it was at the center of the desert, and the battle is centered around our lives right now. Because of Jesus, we have an example of how to fight against the schemes of the enemy and how to claim our identity with boldness, confidence, and steel in our conviction.

I gave you some negative facts when writing the Know Yourself chapter of this book. My focus on the negative was intentional with the hopes of making you aware of how hard the enemy has worked to keep your true identity hidden under the mounds of junk he has thrown your way. It was my intent to encourage you to spend some extra time getting to know yourself. It is well worth the extra time and effort.

Don't ever underestimate yourself and think you are not worthy enough for God's attention. That is far from the truth; you have significance. In our search for significance we have overlooked the fact that we are significantly made. His intentions for you are far more than you can imagine. You are no accident; you are not a Plan B. You were born to shake a generation from the enemy's snare. If you didn't have a purpose, God would not have allowed you to be born. God fashioned you even before He brought the world into existence. You are a vital part of God's end-time plan of redemption. Not only has He commissioned you in His manifesto, He has also prepared you to accomplish His will and purposes on Earth. Think about this; you are a unique receptacle made especially for the power of God. You carry the Presence of God with you wherever you go (1 Corinthians 3:16).

God needs troops, so suit up, girl! Think about it. You, yes you, were placed in the Kingdom to be part of His end-time army. He even mentioned you in His end-time conquering manifesto (Psalm 68:10).

I love the fact that our Heavenly Father even knows when we lose one hair from our head. Think about that when you have feelings of insignificance. His thoughts for you are amazing. If you don't believe me, read what the Word has to say about His thoughts toward you.

> Oh yes, you shaped me first inside, then out; you formed me in my mother's womb. I thank you, High God—you're breathtaking! Body and soul, I am marvelously made! I worship in adoration— what a creation! You know me inside and out, you know every bone in my body; You know exactly how I was made, bit by bit, how I was sculpted from nothing into something. Like an open book, you watched me grow from conception to birth; all the stages of my life were spread out before you, The days of my life all prepared before I'd even lived one day. Your thoughts—how rare, how beautiful! God, I'll never comprehend them! I couldn't even begin to count them—any more than I could count the sand of the sea.
>
> Psalm 139:13-18, MSG

Hopefully by now you are convinced of your value in the eyes of God, and the fact that you do have a Divine destiny. If you're not there yet, don't quit. You'll get there! Even Jesus had to deal with the accusations of the devil concerning His identity as the Son of God. Satan used the same strategies in the desert to try and take down Jesus that he used in the Garden to take down Eve. He tried to make Jesus doubt God's words. He tried to make Jesus doubt God's intentions for His life with those words. With every doubt Satan tried to instill in Jesus, he began with the question of His identity: "**If you are** the Son of God...." In both the Garden and the desert, Satan knew the words of God and tried to pervert their meanings to manipulate the children of God. He is still trying to do the same with us today. I say it like this, first the Garden, then thousands of years later the desert, and thousands of years later, in your sphere. We need to follow the example of Jesus when the enemy confronted Him in the desert.

Jesus combated what the enemy said with what the scriptures say. He combated what was spoken against Him, with what is written about Him. Like Jesus, we must thwart Satan's tactics of doubt with what we know is certain in God's Word.

You must remember you are unique. Why you are here on Earth is specifically just for you, and so is your purpose. The enemy knows what the Word says about you and who you are. Don't let him know more about your identity than you know about yourself. Here is a list of "Don't Entertain Thoughts" because they are the accusations of your adversary:

- Don't think you don't have a purpose.
- Don't think there is nothing special about yourself.
- Don't believe that purpose belongs only to others.
- Don't entertain the thought that you are Plan B.

Each of us has a Divine purpose and a calling. We each have our own identity and sphere of influence. It is up to each of us to rise to that calling.

President Jimmy Carter said it like this: "I have one life and one chance to make it count for something. My faith demands that I do whatever I can, wherever I am, whenever I can, for as long as I can, with whatever I have, to try to make a difference." SELAH

סֶלָה

SELAH
PAUSE–PONDER–PRAY

PAUSE

You have to do your own growing no matter how tall your grandfather was.[1]

—Abraham Lincoln

PONDER

You were made by God for His pleasure. Until you understand that, life will never make sense to you. This poem by Russell Kelfer says it all:

You are who you are for a reason.
You're part of an intricate plan.
You're a precious and perfect unique design.
Called God's special woman or man.

You look like you look for a reason.
Our God made no mistake.
He knit you together within the womb.
You're just what He wanted to make.

The parents you had were the ones He chose,
And no matter how you may feel,
They were custom-designed with God's plan in mind,

---

[1] https://www.brainyquote.com/quotes/abraham_lincoln_108532.

And they bear the Master's seal.

No, that trauma you faced was not easy
And God wept that it hurt you so;
But it was allowed to shape your heart
So that into His likeness you'd grow.

You are who you are for a reason,
You've been formed by the Master's rod.
You are who you are beloved,
Because there is a God![1]

You owe future generations your testimony of how God helped you fulfill His purposes for your life on Earth. The proof of evidence will continue to speak long after you're in Heaven.

> Write down for coming generations what the Lord has done so that people not yet born will praise him.
>
> Psalm 102:18, TEV

PRAY

Father, I am so glad that You knew me and called me even before I was conceived in my mother's womb. According to Your Word, I am no mistake or a Plan B; You called me, and I ask You to help me to fulfill all that You brought me into this world to do!
I pray this in Jesus' Name. Amen!

---

[1] https://library.timelesstruths.org/music/You_Are_.

CHAPTER 4

Know Your Enemy

Praying Mama: Lois and Eunice

The biblical record of Timothy demonstrates the value of positive Christian training in the home. Lois and Eunice took the responsibility to pass on their faith very seriously, and as a result they raised up a young man to become a servant of Christ. For this, they have gone down in history as outstanding mothers and great women of faith. In 2 Timothy 1:5, the Apostle Paul writes: "I have been reminded of your sincere faith, which first lived in your grandmother Lois and in your mother Eunice and, I am persuaded, now lives in you also."

— Mother and Grandmother of Timothy

> Most importantly, be disciplined and stay on guard. Your enemy the devil is prowling around outside like a roaring lion, just waiting and hoping for the chance to devour someone.
>
> 1 Peter 5:8, TPT

I grew up in the era of World War II and experienced the trauma of telling my daddy goodbye at the bus station, without fully understanding all the ramifications of what was going on. I just knew my daddy was dressed differently, and everyone was sad and crying, because he was leaving to go fight somebody who was mean. I had no understanding of the war we were in, nor the enemy my daddy was going to fight. My understanding was limited. *Someone was trying to kill us (a child's perspective), and my daddy was leaving me to go fight that someone or something.*

Praying Mamas, as God's end-time warriors, we cannot afford to have a child's perspective of our enemy and the war we are currently engaged in. The war we are presently engaged in is crucial to the survival of our families and generations to come. Paul said, "Now we do not want you to be uninformed, believers" (1 Thessalonians 4:13, AMP).

One translation says we do not want you to be ignorant of the devil and his schemes. Everywhere we look we are reminded of the actual battle that exists. The times in which we live often feel desperate and uncertain. The devil and his forces of darkness never wait for us to be ready for their attack. They are ruthless, determined and cunning. Satan could care less if we feel prepared or prayed up, ready for our day; in fact, he would prefer us not to be.

Without doubt, we need to know our enemy and how he operates. However, we need to know our Jesus far better than our enemy. Let me offer some wisdom here. Be careful not to become obsessed with the study of the devil. Far too many Christians spend far too much time thinking about Satan and studying his ways and acts. When you do that, you put yourself in harm's way.

I am not suggesting you should be afraid of the enemy nor stick your head in the sand and pretend he doesn't exist. That would be false teaching on my part. However, I have heard too many well-educated, influential teachers say something to this effect, "If you leave the devil alone and don't involve yourself in all that spiritual warfare jargon, perhaps the devil will leave you alone." I say this respectfully, "That's erroneous teaching."

Read the scenario in Judges 4, the happenings in Jael's home. The enemy ended up in her living room and had the audacity to ask for a place to rest and something to eat. How did that happen? It happened because Jael's husband was a passive fence-sitter. His theory could have been that of noncommittal to either side, neither Israel nor Israel's enemy, King Jabin. He must have been deceived by the false teaching, "If you leave the enemy alone and not engage in battle, he will leave you and your family alone."

The tactics of our enemy haven't changed a bit. I am at a loss for words when I think of the audacity and persistence of Satan trying to gain access to our children's mind. Let's not be naive about the enemy and his strategies. He will use any opportunity or device to invite himself into the living rooms of our homes. Yes, I said, "Our homes, Christian homes." He even has the gall to ask you to pop some popcorn for your children and grandchildren while Harry Potter teaches them about mysticism, witchcraft and all the neat things witches and warlocks can do with their great powers. Praying Mamas, don't be uninformed, little Harry is not just a cute little guy wearing horn-rimmed glasses. His message to your child is lethal. Mamas, wake up, it is time to get out the tent peg as Jael did, and do some housecleaning. We cannot allow our living rooms to become a place of tranquility for the enemy of our children's souls.

Jael was not a fence-sitter. She did not allow popular consensus to influence her. She made a conscientious decision to do something about the set of circumstances she found herself in. She was one of those unsung heroes. Her choice to take the correct position not only saved her family, it also saved her nation.

In this last day war for our prophetic destinies, we cannot afford to be neutral. Neutralism is an open invitation for the enemy to enter your home and bring havoc to both you and your family. We will never be able to change families, schools, cities, nor the nations by being fence-sitters. We must engage in the present war set against God and our families.

You and I cannot benefit by playing both sides against the middle. In other words, you cannot favor both opponents to ensure personal victory in the battle. Neutrality is a detriment to our families. We must be on the side of God and on the side of His Word.

I really think the following story out of Aesop's Fables shows us a true picture of trying to be neutral with our enemy:

The Laborer and the Snake

A snake, having made his hole close to the porch of a cottage, inflicted a mortal bite on the cottager's infant son. Grieving over his loss, the father resolved to kill the snake. The next day, when it came out of its hole for food, he took up his axe, but by swinging too hastily, missed its head and cut off only the end of its tail. After some time the cottager, afraid that the Snake would bite him also, endeavored to make peace, and placed some bread and salt in the hole. The snake, slightly hissing, said, "There can henceforth be no peace between us; for whenever I see you, I shall remember the loss of my tail, and whenever you see me you will be thinking of the death of your son." No one truly forgets injuries in the presence of him who caused the injury.[1]

For thousands of years, soldiers have been taught this principle of war, "to defeat your enemy you must know your enemy." If you go into a battle blind, with no knowledge of the army who is coming against you, you should expect to be defeated. The military teaches that the better you know your enemy, the way he operates, the way he attacks, and the kinds of weapons he uses, the more you will be prepared to win the conflict with him.

In Ephesians 6, Paul concludes his letter to the church of Ephesus as he begins to speak about spiritual warfare and depicts the Christian life as a battleground. He introduces our enemy and tells us five facts about him.

> Now my beloved ones, I have saved these most important truths for last: Be supernaturally infused with strength through your life-union with the Lord Jesus. Stand victorious with the force of his explosive power flowing in and through you. Put on God's complete set of armor provided for us, so that you will be

[1] Translated by George Fyler Townsend, *Aesop's Fables*, Amazon Digital Services, Inc., p. 25.

protected as you fight against the evil strategies of the accuser! Your hand-to-hand combat is not with human beings, but with the highest principalities and authorities operating in rebellion under the heavenly realms. For they are a powerful class of demon-gods and evil spirits that hold this dark world in bondage. Because of this, you must wear all the armor that God provides so you're protected as you confront the slanderer, for you are destined for all things and will rise victorious.

Ephesians 6:10-13, TPT

In this passage, Paul informs us that our enemy is evil and gives us five facts about him:

1. The enemy leader is Satan.
2. The enemy is a spirit being.
3. The enemy has many allies.
4. The enemy uses many tactics.
5. The enemy is out to destroy you.

We must realize, when we face conflict and warfare, we are not dealing with human beings. We are not in a natural conflict, we are in a spiritual conflict.

> We live in the flesh—in the natural world. But our warfare is not in the natural world. Our warfare is in the spirit. We are not wrestling or fighting against physical forces that we can see or touch with our natural senses. They are invisible. We are in one-on-one combat with evil spirits, principalities, powers, world rulers of darkness

and hosts of spiritual wickedness in the atmosphere that surrounds this earth.[1]

Let me summarize what you just read, Satan is the ultimate enemy; he is a spiritual enemy, and he has enlisted all kinds of spiritual allies to help him in this ensuing war. All of these beings are out to destroy anyone who is created in the image of God. They have many ways and means of doing this. We are in the middle of the conflict of the ages. Sometimes, the battles are often simple things that we may not recognize as warfare. Not all attacks of the enemy are obvious. Most likely many of his assignments against you and your family are subtle. Looking closely at Nehemiah and the rebuilding of the wall in Jerusalem, we are able to understand eight specific ways in which Satan tried to stop Nehemiah from rebuilding the wall. I will list them for you, but you need to meditate on Nehemiah, chapters four through six. Read and meditate on these chapters in several translations. You may well recognize some of these tactics at work in your own life. The assignments against Nehemiah and the Jews were as follows:

- anger
- ridicule and intimidation
- war, threats of physical attack and confusion
- division among yourselves
- the temptation to compromise or reason with the world
- exhaustion
- fear/fear of man.[2]

It should give you confidence knowing Nehemiah and the Jews overcame their enemies then, and we, through Jesus, can overcome the same enemies now. If you study the passage closely, they overcame their enemies by prayer, perseverance,

---

[1] We God's Victorious Army Bible Spiritual Warfare/Reference Edition II, p. 1118.
[2] Dakes Reference Bible; Chapter 4:1-2, p. 501.

constant readiness for battle, and most importantly, God working alongside them. They were never alone in their battle.

Even with all that interference, the wall was soon finished.

> It was the 25th day of Elul. The work had been accomplished in 52 days. When our enemies heard the work was complete and the surrounding nations saw our wall, their confidence crumbled. Only one possible conclusion could be drawn: it was not just our efforts that had done this thing. God had been working alongside us.
>
> Nehemiah 6:15,16, The Voice Bible, (emphasis mine)

In Romans, Paul encourages the Roman believers:

> Yet in all things we are more than conquerors and gain an overwhelming victory through Him who loved us [so much that He died for us].
>
> Romans 8:37, AMP

You, Praying Mamas, have a Nehemiah anointing. You are the Nehemiah of your family and the generations to come. You will rebuild the ruins and rubble of what the enemy has tried to destroy in your tribe.

Reading the story of Nehemiah's rebuilding of the wall in Jerusalem should encourage you. Yes, they fought many battles in the process, but they continued to call upon their one true God and never let their enemy's distractions muddle their focus on rebuilding the wall. Nehemiah knew his God, his enemy, and his own true identity. The enemy tried identity theft on Nehemiah and the Jews, but it didn't work. We too must be determined not to abort our assignments and get off the wall, no matter how heated the battle becomes. I am convinced this story would have a different ending if Nehemiah's relationship with God had been an apathetic one.

As I conclude this chapter, I will list three things the enemy does not want you to know about him. Satan's threat may seem real and fierce, but he is not all powerful. He wants to be, and he wants you to believe he is; he is the great pretender. His greatest aspiration is to have a title or position like God has, but that will never be. The Bible tells us differently.

There are things Satan would prefer you not know about him because it reveals his weaknesses:

1. The enemy can't be everywhere at the same time.
    He has evil forces at work for him, but he is limited in what he can do and where he can be.
2. The enemy is not able to be in full control.
    His power is limited, and his destination is certain, so he seeks to take as many with him into destruction as he possibly can, knowing full well that his time is limited.
3. The enemy does not know all.
    If he does not know all, he cannot read our minds, nor does he possess the power to have the full knowledge that God has.

He can overhear our conversations, even to ourselves. He observes our behavior, decisions and knows our weaknesses. We inform him with our own mouths. We should stay very aware that he is studying our life and the lives of our children. He can predict our responses based on past decisions. You can be sure that the enemy uses any of our shortcomings to his advantage, but he still does not know what God knows.

Most definitely, you must know God and His character. You need to fully understand who you are and your purpose in life. And yes, you need not be ignorant of your enemy and his schemes. I challenge you to know your enemy, but know your Jesus far better. For every one look at Satan, take ten looks at Jesus; that's a good ratio.

סֶלָה

SELAH
PAUSE–PONDER–PRAY

PAUSE

Courage is a remarkable quality. With it, nothing and nobody can stand in your way. Without it, others will define your path forward. Without it, you are at the mercy of life's temptations. Without courage, men will be ruled by tyrants and despots. Without courage, no great society can flourish. Without courage, the bullies of the world rise up. With it, you can accomplish any goal. With it, you can defy and defeat evil.

> You must rise above your fears, your doubts, and your fatigue. No matter how dark it gets, you must complete the mission. This is what separates you from everyone else.[1]

PONDER

The song "Praise The Lord" sums it up so well.

> When you're up against a struggle that shatters all your dreams
> And your hopes have been cruelly crushed by Satan's manifested schemes
> And you feel the urge within you to submit to earthly fears

---

[1] McRaven, William H. *Make Your Bed*, p. 68-69. Grand Central Publishing. Kindle Edition.

Don't let the faith you're standing in seem to disappear

Now Satan is a liar and he wants to make us think
That we are paupers when he knows himself
we're children of the King
So lift up the mighty shield of faith for the battle
must be won
We know that Jesus Christ has risen so the
work's already done

Praise the Lord, He can work through those who
praise Him
Praise the Lord, for our God inhabits praise
Praise the Lord, for the chains that seem to bind
you
Serve only to remind you that they drop
powerless behind you
When you praise Him[1]

PRAY
Dear Heavenly Father, I need courage to fight against the devil, against terrors and troubles, temptations, attractions, darkness and weariness, depression, and above all fear. Grant me the power of Your Holy Spirit to persevere and the courage to fight until the battle is won for Your Kingdom's sake.
I pray this in Jesus' Name. Amen!

---

[1] Songwriters: Elliott B. Bannister/Michael Vincent Hudson, *Praise The Lord* lyrics © Warner/Chappell Music, Inc.

CHAPTER 5

Tag You're It

Praying Mama: Eliza Spurgeon

"There was a boy once—a very sinful child—who hearkened not to the counsel of his parents. But his mother prayed for him, and now he stands to preach to this congregation every Sabbath. And when his mother thinks of her firstborn preaching the Gospel, she reaps a glorious harvest that makes her a glad woman." Before her son was the The Prince of Preachers, he was a young boy in the arms of a godly mother.

— Mother of Charles Spurgeon

From the days of John the Baptist until now the kingdom of heaven suffereth violence, and the violent take it by force.

Matthew 11:12, KJV

To be honest with you, I never liked reading this scripture. It did not meet the criteria of what I expected in my journey as a Christian. Yes, I fought battles. As a wife and mother, most of my battles were what I call "The Barbie® Wars of Life." For example, out of spite, my friend's little girl cut the hair off my little girl's Barbie doll. The reason? Because she didn't have one like it. Now, that is a war I got involved in, and I was justified in doing so. You don't mess with my child's Barbie; the Mama Bear will arise in me.

I didn't like the wording of the scripture "forcefully" and "violent people" fighting an enemy over the Kingdom of God. I had too much to do and too many places to go to get involved in a ferocious, face-to-face encounter with the enemy. Let someone else do it. I don't want to be involved in bloody, violent combat. Taking something by force sounded like a lot of hard work and conflict. I was already involved in Barbie Wars. How much more can a fearsome warrior take?

It wasn't until the birth of our oldest grandson, Brandon, that I realized how much the devil desires to kill our righteous seed and future generations. All of a sudden, my Barbie Wars were no longer of importance. Out of nowhere, the real battle had started. What was to be a joyful event in our lives quickly evolved into a life or death situation. The enemy wanted the life of our righteous seed! Satan is a ruthless killer, lying in wait for any opportunity to strike.

I was standing by my daughter's side in the labor room when, unexpectedly, the fetal monitor activated and was doing strange things. With every contraction, the heartbeat of our baby dropped extremely low, showing signs of distress. I knew we were in major trouble and alerted the nurses. They quickly prepared my daughter for emergency delivery. Our first-born grandson was in danger of cardiac arrest because his umbilical cord was wrapped around his neck numerous times, and he was stuck in the birth canal.

In the midst of this attack, I thought I was going to faint. The Bible tells us, "If we faint in the day of adversity, our strength is small" (Proverbs 24:10, ASV). I taught that very scripture many times in my Bible study groups. It was easy to teach, but hard to walk out when you're in violent warfare with your back against the wall.

Stunned, my husband and I stood in the hall looking at each other with a helpless gaze. Our daughter and grandchild's lives were in jeopardy. My dress was stained from my daughter's vomit brought on by birthing stress. Her baby was too large for the birthing canal and hung there with his umbilical cord wrapped around his neck, dying.

The accuser, our enemy, showed no mercy. Immediately, he began throwing accusations at us. He gave us no time to get our military bearings and grab our Bible to renew our strength. The lives of our seed were in danger; guerrilla warfare was inevitable, with no time to strategize. We had to wield the Sword of the Lord quickly in order to save the life of our seed. I was accustomed to Barbie Wars, but this battle was bloody and violent. Now I had an understanding of the phrase "Take It By Force." There was no chance for us to go AWOL; we were in a battle like it or not.

All of our Bible college training was lost in the whirlwind of the battle when we heard our son-in-law cry out from the delivery room, "Pray! Pray! Pray!"

Yes, with the scurry of the nurses and doctors and our son-in-law's cry for help, fear tried to paralyze us. I am not sure what my husband was doing because the realization suddenly hit me that the only hope for the life of my daughter and grandson was to wield the Sword of the Lord. I tried to pull warfare scriptures from my memory bank. All I could come up with was "Your hand is not short."

I kept repeating, "Your hand is not short." I envisioned His arm extending down to my daughter and her baby. His hand touching the two of them in their time of distress. The complete scripture reads like this:

> Behold the LORD'S hand is not so short that it cannot save, Nor His ear so impaired that it cannot hear.
>
> Isaiah 59:1, AMP

Praying Mama, you don't have to have a master's degree in theology to declare the Word of God. The Word is alive, active and powerful, sharper than a two-edged sword. It will stand on its own merits. We had to stand and let the Word do the work for us. "Your hand is not short" was all it took to save the life of my daughter and my oldest grandson!

Our grandson, Brandon, his wife and two beautiful daughters just visited us. Each time I see him, I cannot help but give thanks to God for His mercy to a young mother who could only say, "Your hand is not short." Each time I see my grandson and watch him enjoy life with his beautiful wife and children, I witness the evidence of God's faithfulness to His Word and the cry of a young mother who had only fought in Barbie Wars. I seize that Selah moment to reflect on God's integrity.

As parents, we are in a spiritual battle with an enemy who does not believe in fighting fair. He is a destroyer and liar. As an army, we cannot allow him to intimidate us with his fear tactics.

In every major battle, both spiritual and natural, the army that wins must have a mindset of a victor. Sun Tzu, the Chinese general and strategist, said this in his book, *The Art of War.*

> To win the war, you must be prepared to win every battle on every front.[1]

In every major season, God has always amassed an army of mighty men and women who are not afraid to get in the trenches and fight the enemy. Many times, they use Satan's own military guerrilla tactics. These fearsome warriors take him down and advance God's kingdom.

Recently, I noticed a sign in front of an area school. It was the last day of school and the beginning of summer vacation. The caption was: "Parents: Tag You're It!"

The sign caught my eye because I was in the process of writing this chapter, Tag Your It, featuring Praying Mamas.

Months ago, while meditating on possible chapter titles, the Lord brought to my mind a game we played as kids, Tag You're It. He said, "I am currently tagging mothers and including them in my end-time, victorious army." Until I studied the flow of the game, I couldn't fully grasp what the Lord was saying to me and how the game could possibly be applicable to Praying Mamas.

---

[1] Wikiquote **https://en.wikiquote.org/wiki/Sun_Tzu**. Accessed February 28, 2019.

The flow of the game is as follows: One person is "It," and they are required to touch someone else. When you are touched by the person who is "It," you immediately become "It." Now, it's your turn to tag someone else. The game usually continues until everyone decides to stop, or until a predetermined number of people have become "It."[1]

You may think I'm hard pressed to get a spiritual connotation out of this game, but I know what the Lord said to me.

As kids, when we played the game, we would look for that specific person to tag. When that individual was tagged, we would yell, "Tag you're it!" That was an authoritative declaration identifying that person as "It." The proclamation identified them as part of the current activity.

If you understand the jargon of social media, by tagging someone, you are identifying and informing them that you want them to be a part of a current happening. You may want to pause here and make a mental note. You can untag yourself at any time. God may tag you for an assignment, but He will never require you to do anything against your will. He is not a dictator.

God Himself is looking for mothers whom He can tag to be part of His end-time prayer movement. This group of powerful, warring women, is being amassed from all parts of the world. You can rest assured God would never tag an individual without giving strength and grace to accomplish what He asks of them.

> The eyes of the Lord run to and fro throughout the earth to show himself strong in behalf of those whose hearts are blameless toward him.
> 2 Chronicles 16:9, KJV, (emphasis mine)

In military terms, an army is assembled one person at a time in order to achieve its common cause. The purpose of an army is

---

[1] Wikipedia https://en.wikipedia.org/wiki/Tag_(game).

to protect and defend nations from a cruel enemy who is at work seeking those he can destructively afflict and take over their domain. His strategy to occupy the land begins with a master plan to capture the family.

In the natural, the President of the United States is the Commander in Chief of the armed forces and responsible for all final decisions. In spiritual wars, our Commander in Chief is the King of Glory; Jesus is His name. He is mighty in battle and has the final say of all armies, both in Heaven and on Earth.

> The Lord stands in full authority to shatter to pieces the kings who stand against you on the day he displays his terrible wrath. He will judge every rebellious nation, filling their battlefield with corpses, and will shatter the strongholds of ruling powers.
>
> Psalm 110:5-6, TPT

Who is this King with full authority? Psalm 24 makes clear the answer:

> Who is [He then] this King of glory? The Lord of hosts, He is the King of glory [who rules over all creation with His heavenly armies].
>
> Psalm 24:10, AMP

Praying Mama, we are not alone in this battle. Our Commander in Chief is mighty in battle. He can be trusted to never steer us wrong, lead us astray, or forsake us in battle. We have moved from the season of Barbie Wars to an era of guerrilla warfare, which will require a violent faith to win.

Mothers are arising all around the world who are being tagged by God Himself to ferociously fight for their children and communities. These Warrior Mamas will not be fighting alone but will be standing in the strength of the King of Glory who fights alongside them.

Praying Mamas, I declare, "It's your time to rise." You are the Rising Stars of this new era. Don't wait for the future; build the future on your knees. You are paving the way for breakthrough and supernatural restoration of your righteous seed and their future.

If you are reading this book, listen closely with your spiritual ears. Perhaps you will hear the voice of the Father declare, "TAG YOU'RE IT," identifying you as a vital part of the prayer movement of Praying Mamas. I reiterate: "Where there's a praying mother, there's always hope."

TAG YOU'RE IT!

NOTE:
Charles Haddon Spurgeon was an English Particular Baptist preacher. Spurgeon remains highly influential among Christians of various denominations, among whom he is known as the "Prince of Preachers". His name has been, and still is, known around the world. Crowds flocked to his church to hear him preach. When he died, 60,000 admirers filed past his casket and 100,000 lined his funeral route. Even today, people visit his grave to pay tribute. He warned, "We shall soon have to handle truth, not with kid gloves, but with gauntlets–the gauntlets of holy courage and integrity. Go on, ye warriors of the cross, for the King is at the head of you."[1]

---

[1] **https://en.wikipedia.org/wiki/Charles_Spurgeon**. Accessed February 27, 2019.

סֶלָה

SELAH
PAUSE–PONDER–PRAY

PAUSE

> There is no neutral ground in the universe; every
> square inch, ever split second, is claimed by God
> and counter-claimed by Satan.
>
> — C.S. Lewis

PONDER

The generations to come need to see you, Praying Mama, not
only rising up out of the state of oppression and depression,
being all shiny and cute; they need to see the furiousness of a
Mama Bear whose cubs are missing or endangered. The power
of a mother is neither here nor there, it's the ferociousness of a
mother if you mess with her cubs. Just ask a mother bear.

> Like a bear whose cubs have been taken away, I
> will tear out your heart. I will devour you like a
> hungry lioness and mangle you like a wild animal.
>
> Hosea 13:8, NLT

Alexander the Great said, "I am not afraid of an army of lions
led by a sheep, I am afraid of an army of sheep led by a lion."

**Angelic assignments given to bring in the seed of Praying
Mothers!**

In the Spirit I saw a heavenly rush of Angels gathering. Prayers of mothers crying out for their children seemed to have gathered momentum. These prayers, as though being amplified in the Spirit, were pounding, relentlessly shaking the door hinges of Heaven. Heaven itself had been shaken by these violent prayers as though a bear had been robbed of its cubs.

Prophetic word given by Bill Yount[1]

PRAY

Father, I thank You that You saw fit to Tag me to be a part of Your end-time manifesto. I know that the enemy wouldn't be fighting so hard against us, if we weren't making a difference for Your Kingdom. Fill me with the power of Your Holy Spirit. LORD, remind me that the battle belongs to You, and whatever we're up against can be taken down in one swoop by Your Mighty Hand.

I pray this in Jesus' Name. Amen!

---

[1] **http://billyount.blogspot.com/2015/07**. Accessed February 28, 2019.

CHAPTER 6

The Wild Ox Anointing

Praying Mama: Betsy Moody

Betsy Moody is an example of perseverance. She is an exemplary illustration to every single mom, who longs to raise children for God without a father. "Trust in God" was her simple creed. She could not give her children a theological education, but she had the reality of that theology. God was using a mother to train a humble, lowly servant, who stood in amazement when the crowds came out to hear him. She was training a servant who would not touch the Glory.

— Mother of Dwight L. Moody

Where no oxen are, the grain crib is empty, but much increase [of crops], comes by the strength of the ox.

Proverbs 14:4, AMP

As I stated earlier in the book, I was born in the era of World War II. I can still recall the emotions I experienced when I walked by an Army recruiting office. Without fail, my eyes would catch a glimpse of a poster in the window which depicted a very determined looking man, declaring in bold letters, "I WANT YOU FOR THE U.S. ARMY". The letters were dark blue, outlined with red; the 'YOU' was solid red with a larger font. This 1917 large printed picture was used to recruit soldiers for both World War I and

World War II.[1] The depiction didn't cause me to fear, but it did make an impression on my soul. It was evident, people are needed in the time of war, and there is no other recourse.

In his book, *Prayer Is Invading The Impossible*, Jack Hayford wrote:

> Perhaps the high point of Jesus' teaching ministry came when His disciples asked Him, "Lord teach us to pray." In response, Jesus taught them nothing of mysticism, nothing of religious pretense, nothing of meditation, nothing of bizarre physical contortions, nor anything of memorized incantations attended by clouds of incense.
>
> But He did teach them something about a matter of violence. He was very clear on that one thing. Prayer was a matter of assault, binding and warfare invasion.
>
> While on Earth, He taught that things may appear impossible, yet from the Heaven side of things, violence can explode the impossible. However, it needs troops for the invasion.[2]

Jesus emphasized that troops are needed for the incursion of things impossible. If we look at human culture, from Earth's view, we can easily ascertain that things appear impossible. Commercial sex trafficking is a very real threat to millions of children around the world. Children account for nearly one-third of identified trafficking victims globally.[3]

---

[1] https://www.washingtonpost.com/.../the-uncle-sam-i-want-you- poster- is-100-years-old. Accessed 03/28/2019.

[2] Jack Hayford, *Prayer Is Invading The Impossible*; p.27, 28.

[3] **https://www.unicef.org/stories/children-make-almost-one-third-all-human-trafficking-victims-worldwide**. Accessed 03/28/2019.

Children between the ages of 7 and 13 are vulnerable to child sexual assault. According to USA Today, depression and teen suicide are soaring.[1]

Praying Mamas, we cannot afford to look from the Earth side at the behavior of this 21st century culture. We must see and hear what Heaven has to say about it. Jesus taught that a power is available which can violently shatter impossibilities, but you have an assurance from the Holy Spirit.

> You shall receive power (ability, efficiency, and might) when the Holy Spirit has come upon you and you shall be My witnesses in Jerusalem and all Judea and Samaria and to the ends (the bounds of the earth).
>
> Acts 1:8, AMP

Through the Holy Spirit, you have miracle powers within you. We have the promise of Power for Purpose.

Two words used in the New Testament describe the power that God is bestowing upon His Army of Praying Mamas. The two types of power are *exousia* and *dunamis* that translate *authority* and *power*. I like to refer to these two powers as the "Dual anointing or double anointing." It's true, we can't combat the enemy within our own strength; however, we have been given God's power and authority to shatter Satan's strongholds of the impossible.

The word *exousia* is defined as "authority, jurisdiction, capability, absolute power." It is this power that Jesus gave to us in Luke 10:19, when He gave us the authority to tread on serpents, scorpions and over all the power of the enemy.

---

[1] **https://www.usatoday.com/in-depth/news/health/2018/12/06/depression-rates-rise-utah-looking-slow-increase/2213071002**. December 12, 2018. Accessed February 28, 2019.

The word *dunamis* is defined as "miraculous power, ability, strength, and force." It also means "inherent power" or "power possessed."[1]

In Mama terms, God has given us the anointing of a wild ox, which is His own ability and strength, to tag our children and release them into their Divine destiny, freeing them from the enemy's power. What this generation needs is a personal encounter with God and an awareness of who they are in Christ. If we tag this generation, they will become the pursuer. They will in turn tag and influence their peers without their peers influencing them.

It is the desire of our Heavenly Father that each of us receive the Holy Spirit's powerful anointing, in order to have a greater influence in the Kingdom. Remember, God will never order His troops to go to war without giving power and strength to accomplish what He has commissioned them to do.

Several years ago, while in prayer, the Lord spoke to me concerning His last day conquering warriors. He said, "Because of the immensity of the battles and increased opposition, I am anointing my people with a double anointing of strength and power to accomplish what I have commissioned them to do." Because of the escalation of warfare, a greater anointing of strength will be absolutely necessary if we are to rescue future generations from the claws of an unmerciful enemy. I labeled this impartation of strength and power as "The Wild Ox Anointing." The Psalmist David referred to this anointing in Psalm 92:10. He prophetically declared the Ox anointing over himself by decreeing, "I shall be anointed with fresh oil."

In Psalm 92, King David's primary focus was the weapon of worship of his God. We must realize that worship is a powerful weapon in war. King David worshiped his way into the Presence of God before declaring the fresh anointing over himself or the destruction of his enemies.

---

[1] Anoint: Definition from the KJV Dictionary - AV1611.COM, **https://av1611.com/kjbp/kjv-dictionary/anoint.html**. Accessed 03/28/2019.

You, LORD, are on high forever. For behold, Your enemies, O LORD, For behold, Your enemies will perish; All who do evil will be scattered. But my horn [my emblem of strength and power] You have exalted like that of a wild ox; I am anointed with fresh oil [for Your service]. My eye has looked on my foes; My ears hear of the evildoers who rise up against me.

Psalm 92:8-11, AMP

Not only was David a King, he was an anointed warrior. He learned the secret of declaring God's Word over himself. The Bible says he had to encourage himself in the Lord. Mamas, in the battle for your family, you may have to acquire the skill of encouraging yourself in the Lord, by declaring His promises over the circumstances you face when dealing with this generation of young people.

In this Psalm, I believe David worshiped until he felt the Presence of God, before he started to declare.

- He declared that his horn, power and authority is in God.
- I can imagine him putting his hands on his head and declaring, "I am anointed with fresh oil and the Power of the Holy Spirit rests mightily upon me today."
- He continues by touching his eyes and declaring the anointed words in Jeremiah 33:3. "I declare, The Eternal One will show me great things beyond what I can imagine, and things I have never known."
- Finally, he declares that his ears are opened that he might hear the glorious plans of God.

Praying Mama, in this hour you must have a lifestyle of declaring and decreeing God's promises over your finances, health, yourself, your family, your community, and your nation. That is part of our warfare strategy. You need to understand the following two words because they are part of our arsenal of weapons to use against the enemy of our soul and the souls of our children. If we are going to see change in our culture, we must learn the power of declaring and decreeing God's promises.

- **DECLARE:** to make something known
- **DECREE:** Judgment passed with Authority

The Wild Ox Anointing and intercession are used synonymously in conjunction with the coming Harvest. The wild ox is one of the most dangerous and strongest beasts in the animal kingdom. The ferocious lion will flee the fury of the wild ox. What a powerful, prophetic picture of our enemy fleeing from the Presence of King Jesus who resides within us.

The Ox Anointing brings forth great breakthrough. The Ox intercedes and cries out in the evening and the dark hours of the night, while others are peacefully sleeping. The power of this anointing will compel a person to do the work that nobody else wants to do.

What is the connotation of verse ten, when the Psalmist David said, "I am anointed with fresh oil [for Your service]?" Technically speaking, the word anoint has to do with the rubbing or smearing of oil upon someone else. God is the Anointer; there is no other. May I suggest that the Psalmist David was prophetically announcing that a fresh anointing of the Holy Spirit was being infused within himself for service. The believers in the upper room were infused with power when the Holy Spirit was outpoured on the Day of Pentecost. We too need to daily declare, a fresh infusion of the Holy Spirit in order to successfully deal with the giant of impossibles we face in taking the Family Mountain of culture.

Once we spend time in the Presence of Jesus, praising and thanking Him for His power over the enemy, God will suddenly infuse us with fresh oil of great strength and authority equal to that of a wild ox. Once we receive this anointing, all the demonic enemies of God in the spiritual realm will become powerless. They will start to flee before us because of this powerful anointing and the words of authority we decree against them in Jesus' Name.

Holy Spirit further instructed me to make an anointing oil. The word strength and a picture of a wild ox was to be clearly displayed on the label. The instructions concerning the fragrance of the oil was simple, it must have a pungent aroma to match the intensity of the Ox Anointing. His final words were, "My people will require a fresh, new anointing of strength in order to advance the Kingdom of God in the last days." The ox is used as a harvesting animal. Our opening scripture tells us that we will reap an abundant harvest by the strength of the ox.

My husband Sam and I were missionaries to Indonesia and often witnessed the laborious work of the ox as it strained in the heat of the day, plowing the hard, fallow ground and getting it ready for harvest. At night, we would hear the bell of the ox cart as the oxen pulled the extremely heavy load, getting it to its required destination. Without the strength and hard work of the wild ox, there would be no harvest.

Jesus painted a clear prophetic picture of the end-time harvest and its need for workers:

> The harvest is abundant [for there are many who need to hear the good news about salvation], but the workers [those available to proclaim the message of salvation] are few. Therefore, [prayerfully] ask the Lord of the harvest to send out workers, "YOU" into His harvest.
> LUKE 10:2, AMP, (emphasis mine)

Praying Mama, God has need of you. He has tagged you and identified you as part of His violent troops, ready to invade and explode the impossible. In the natural, rescuing a generation from Satan's snares appears impossible. However, God has a group of Spirit-filled, radical mothers who operate with ferocious faith and function in the Wild Ox Anointing. These Mamas are ready to tag, train and equip future generations, pointing them in the direction of their God-given destiny. The Song of Solomon depicts this radical army as fearless and prepared for battle:

> Who is this coming up from the wilderness like a column of smoke, perfumed with myrrh and incense made from all the spices of the merchant? Look! It is Solomon's carriage, escorted by sixty warriors, the noblest of Israel, all of them wearing the sword, all experienced in battle, each with his sword at his side, prepared for the terrors of the night.
>
> Song of Solomon 3:6-8, NIV

The Message Bible portrays this army as Israel's finest, all of them trained for battle, ready for anything, anytime. This radical army of Praying Mamas will never abandon their assignment, retreat, back down or give up.

> Arise and thresh, O daughter of Zion; For I will make your horn iron, and your hoofs bronze.
>
> Micah 4:13, MSG

Because of your tenacity and ferocious faith, a monumental harvest is coming to you, your family, community, and nation. Your oxen's crib will overflow, and restoration will happen in your home. The prodigals are coming home!

NOTE:
Because of a Praying Mama, Dwight L. Moody evangelized throughout the world. In America, he often preached in major cities and at various universities. His heart was for his schools and he spent much of his time in Northfield. Moody was a

visionary who always seemed a step ahead of the status quo. From training women, to reaching out to lost children, to bridging the gap between denominations, he was unlike any other.

סֶלָה

SELAH
PAUSE–PONDER–PRAY

PAUSE

> What kind of people do they think we are? Is it possible they do not realize that we shall never cease to persevere against them until they have been taught a lesson which they and the world will never forget?[1]
>
> —Winston Churchill

PONDER

YOU will be known as God's mighty, militant, military machine, with the Wild Ox Anointing, which the world has never seen nor will ever see again. YOU will be absolutely, totally free, spirit, soul, and body. YOU are made ready by the Spirit for this end-time period in order to fulfill every prophecy concerning God's people. YOU are well equipped for such spiritual warfare such as this world has never seen. Power and dominion are given to YOU by Jehovah God, and absolutely nothing will be able to stand before YOU. YOU are a driving force to be reckoned with in these last days.

The song, *You're an Army*, clearly depicts what YOU are all about.

You're an army dressed for battle - Take the land

---

1 Winston Churchill, https://www.brainyquote.com/quotes/winston_churchill_414116. Accessed February 28, 2019.

The weapons of our warfare
They are mighty through our God
We cut off the giant's head
We eat giants for our bread![1]

With the strength of a wild ox, God led Israel out of Egypt. No magic charms can work against them—just look what God has done for his people. They are like angry lions ready to attack; and they won't rest until their victim is gobbled down.

Numbers 23:22-24, CEV

PRAY

Father, hearken unto me as I call upon You today. Thank You, that I am armed with your power and will advance from victory to victory, crushing the oppression and wickedness of my enemies. Help me to ever be mindful that it is not by my strength that I succeed but by the Might and Strength of Your Holy Spirit that resides within me. I give You praise, and declare that I am anointed with fresh oil and I am armed and battle ready this day. In Jesus' Name I pray, Amen!

On the Next Page I have added a powerful set of decrees and prayers that you can Pray over yourself to cover you with Strength!

---

[1] Rick Pino, **https://genius.com/Rick-pino-youre-an-army-lyrics**. Accessed February 28, 2019.

COVENANT DECREE FOR STRENGTH

Psalm 92:10

But my horn (emblem of excessive strength and stately grace) You have exalted like that of a wild ox; I am anointed with fresh oil. *(Psalms 92:10-Amplified Bible)*

Heavenly Father, in the Name of Jesus I come to you. I want to thank you for the Name of Jesus and the Blood of Jesus. For it is in His Name and by His Blood that I overcome the evil one.

(Spend some time here thanking Him for the Blood, anointing yourself and applying the Blood to your SPIRIT, SOUL, and BODY.)

Declare you are anointed in every aspect of your being.

Father, thank you for the Holy Spirit who dwells within <u>ME</u> to strengthen <u>ME</u> and empower <u>ME</u> to do the work of your Kingdom. Father, your Word says:

"...... if the Spirit of Him who raised Jesus from the dead dwells in you, He who raised Christ from the dead will also give life to your mortal bodies through His Spirit who dwells in you." *(Romans 8:11) NKJV*

DECLARATION FOR STRENGTH:

In Jesus Name, Quicken me according to your Word!
(Anoint your forehead with your OIL)

    * I declare, "The same Spirit that raised Jesus from the dead dwells in ME and He is giving life (strength) to ME right now".

* I Declare that MY HORN (MY emblem of excessive Strength) you have exalted (given ME power) like that of a wild ox.

* I declare, "I am anointed with fresh oil".

Father, your word says, "Where no oxen are, the grain crib is empty, but much increase [of crops] comes by the strength of the ox."

* I declare, "I am a wild ox in the Spirit and I have the strength of the Ox".

* I declare that my grain crib is not empty and I have much increase in my spiritual crop, my financial crop, and my family is blessed in every aspect of their lives.

Holy Spirit, I receive the strength of the ox right now. For it is by you that I am empowered with the life of Christ for this new season.

It is in the name of Jesus I declare this! Amen

CHAPTER 7

Taking Our Families For God

Praying Mama: Dorothy May Skaggs

I'm sure proud to call her my momma. She was as tough as a boot, and soft as cotton all at the same time. My mother was such a powerful prayer warrior. She knew how to pray, and she knew how to believe in what she prayed for. That's as important as praying: If you don't believe, you won't receive. She prayed for me all my life. She prayed that God would make my gift of music a blessing to others and that Jesus would get the Glory for it, not me. I do believe her prayers are still alive, and many of them yet to be fulfilled.[1]

— Mother of Ricky Lee Skaggs

> We will cry out to You in our distress, and You will hear and save us.
>
> 2 Chronicles, 20:9 AMP

Family is big to God. Every person born on the face of Earth was created to be part of His family. Throughout the Bible, God's blueprint for building families is evident. Actually, if you think about it, God really didn't need a family; He desired a family.

Let's face it, anything God loves, Satan loathes. Without doubt, his goal has always been, and still is, to thwart God's plan

---

[1] Ricky Skaggs, *Kentucky Traveler*, itbooks; youritbooks.com, p.222.

for our family. However, God came up with a better plan. He gave His Son for the restoration of His beloved children. He is still supernaturally bringing families back together; it doesn't matter how dysfunctional they may appear. Perhaps, the enemy has tried to convince you that it's too late for your family. I emphatically say this, "It is best to start early, but it is never too late."

Several years ago, our friend, Stephen Wilson, sent me statistics concerning one of the most repeated topics in the Bible. Apostle Wilson said this, "I learned this the first time I read through the Bible after becoming a Grandpa." (I had read it through many times before and not seen this.) God is a God of generations. He is always thinking generationally. Some of the words which speak of generations directly or indirectly appear over 4,000 times in scripture.

- Generation or Generations
- Seed
- Descendants
- Children's children
- House (In reference to descendants)
- Son's sons
- Heirs

He concluded with this statement, "We must always live in such a way as to change our generations for the better. Every decision I make, whether good or bad, affects my generations. My obedience today defines a prophetic future for my most awesome grandchildren."

In recent years, Bible scholars studied and taught on the seven facets of society and how to transform nations. The consensus of the study is as follows, "In order to truly transform a culture with the Gospel of Jesus Christ, the following seven entities of society must be reached. Most religious scholars refer to these entities as the seven mountains of culture: Religion,

Family, Education, Government, Media, Arts and Entertainment and Business.

I mentioned the seven mountains because one of the mountains is the Family Mountain which is the fundamental unit of society. It bears repeating that families have been under constant and prolonged attack because Satan knows the building block of any functioning church, community or nation is the family.

The strategies of the enemy are easily recognized: fatherlessness, divorce (50% rate in secular and Christian marriages), abuse, homosexual marriage, pornography, and other negative influences that have brought great dysfunction to the family.

I am convinced the last day outpouring of the Holy Spirit begins in the home and restoration of the family unit. With the healing of families, conquering the other six mountains will be a much easier task. Strong families generate strong churches. Strong churches impact and produce strong communities. Strong communities influence a nation.

The Bible makes it clear that in the last days, the hearts of parents, especially fathers, will be turned to the children and the children to the fathers (Malachi 4:6).

In his book, *The Orphan Heart*, my friend Larry Burden wrote this statement which is so relevant to family restoration:

> We have a unique opportunity to redirect the course of History. We can redeem the time and reverse the curse of fatherlessness in our spheres of influence. We must never underestimate the authority and power that we have been given as fathers and mothers to shape the destinies of our offspring. For each son and daughter who knows his or her identity and purpose, there is one less orphan wandering aimlessly in life. We must assume our responsibility as fathers and mothers

of faith and shift the future of generations and the future course of the nation.[1]

God is calling fathers and mothers, both spiritual and biological, to bring order to the havoc the enemy has unleashed upon families. He also wants to bring healing to marriages and relationships within families in order to establish a righteous foundation for future generations to stand upon.

As we encounter the enemies that are coming against our families, we must keep in mind Genesis 1:28. God gave us the mandate to take dominion over the Family Mountain; this is our authoritative order from God. We must not only have strategies to follow through with this mandate, we must also recognize that our ultimate Commander is ready and willing to provide us with strategy to take dominion. No wonder demonic forces attack us so heavily when we intercede for the Family Mountain. If we are praying with the Holy Spirit's miracle-working power and strategy, we are announcing Satan's demise and reclaiming the territory. He will not go down without a fight and that is precisely why we must have a plan of attack that is Heaven-sent.

Praying Mamas, because of past failures, you may ask, "How can I pray, when I know I've failed God?" Satan knows well that the awareness of our failures, or even a remote memory of them, can haunt our souls, destroying all our confidence to pray effectually. Don't forget, God's Word has labeled the enemy of our soul as the accuser, as well as the adversary. If we allow him to do so, he will hound our mind with added suggestions of unworthiness and hopelessness when we pray. He will suggest to you that you've botched it up so badly, you cannot possibly expect to intercede for a lost generation. Just remember, your Commander is not only the King of Glory, He is also the God of Grace. We must move past our failures and enter into the place of victory if we expect to transform the family culture.

---

[1] Larry L. Burden, *The Orphan Heart*, Insight International, Inc., p.70.

God wants to eradicate your past in order for you to become who you were destined to be.

For several years I taught in a women's prison. I could readily see the transformation that took place when these women accepted Jesus into their lives. Their favorite song was *Use Me*. The lyrics go like this:

> If You can use anything Lord You can use me
> If You can use anything Lord You can use me
> Take my hands, Lord and my feet
> Touch my heart, Lord and speak through me
> If You can use anything Lord You can use me.[1]

They sang with such passion. I was convinced that God is not looking for perfection, just availability and willingness of heart.

If you read Joshua, chapter two, a harlot's family was saved because she was available and had the audacity to ask that when the city would be taken over, not only would she be saved, but her family as well. She hid the two spies from the king's men, and because she helped them, they responded to her plea to protect her entire family. She wasn't content with just her own salvation, but her desire was for her whole family to be saved. This unreligious woman just taught us a valuable lesson in intercession, "Just Ask."

The first step in seeing ALL your family brought into the Kingdom of God is to believe it is God's will to liberate them. Satan's main strategy is to try to deceive you, with the lie that it must not be God's will to save all your tribe. He will try to convince you that your children, this generation, are such transgressors, even God with His redeeming grace cannot save them. If you listen to those lies, you will never have the faith to see God's hand of mercy at work in your tribe.

It is the will of God for all your family to be saved! My mainstay scripture for the salvation of my household is Acts 16:31:

---

[1] Ron Kenoly, *Use Me,* lyrics.com.

Believe on the Lord Jesus Christ, and thou shalt
be saved and thy house.

Believe me, many opportunities have arisen where I had to refute
Satan's lies and the fear that some of my clan would not be saved.
The Word of God says, "If we believe, not only will we be saved
but our households as well."

God wants you to believe that He desires to save your
family. In Acts 11:14 we read:

> He will give you a message that will rescue both
> you and your household.
>> The Voice Bible

Here again the Bible tells us, "All thy house shall be saved."
Another scripture confirmation for household salvation is in the
Book of John:

> So the father knew that it was at the same hour,
> in the which Jesus said unto him, Thy son liveth:
> and himself believed, and HIS WHOLE
> HOUSE.
>> John 4:53, (emphasis mine)

Nehemiah told God's people to "FIGHT FOR THEIR
FAMILIES."

> Do not be afraid of these people! Instead,
> remember the Eternal, our great and awesome
> Lord. Fight for your people: your sisters and your
> brothers, your sons and your daughters, your
> wives and your homes.
>> Nehemiah 4:14, The Voice Bible

I like the last part of verse 20 in this same chapter. Nehemiah
told the people, "Be assured our True God will fight for us."

Praying Mamas, we cannot afford to get distracted in our quest for our family's restoration. In the early nineties, I heard the following testimony of a Pink Pig Vision which has stayed with me throughout the years. It is so relevant in spiritual warfare. Over the years, I have shared it with many, both old and young alike.

I don't recall all the logistics of names and places, but the illustration is still very vivid in my mind. It taught me to stay focused and not let the little things distract me when God gives me an assignment.

Pink Pig Vision
The gentleman who experienced the visitation said God woke him up in the middle of the night with a vision. In the vision, he was going down the expressway of his city when suddenly God pointed out to him a picture of a little pink pig on a very large billboard.

When he saw the little pink pig, he began to quote pig scriptures. "Don't cast your pearls before swine." He began thinking, "They would trample under their feet God's Word."

When he had finished all his pig scriptures, puzzled about the meaning of the vision, he asked Jesus, "What are you saying to me?"

Jesus addressed him by his first name, and asked, "What did the sign say?" He answered Jesus with a rhetorical question, "What sign? I don't remember a sign, all I saw was a little pink pig."

Jesus said to him, "The sign said, 'DON'T GET DISTRACTED.'" He continued, "That is what my church is doing, looking at little pink pigs and missing the big things I am saying and doing."

This is the era of conquering and the restoration of all things. God wants us to fight in the Spirit for our families. Rahab's heart was quickened to ask and believe for the salvation of her entire family. May God, in turn, challenge our hearts to fight and believe for the salvation of our loved ones.

Praying Mama, as an act of faith, declare right now that families around the world will be restored, starting with your own. Joel 2:25-26 is your linchpin scripture:

> "I will restore to you the years that the locust has eaten, the cankerworm, and the caterpillar, and the palmer worm, my great army which I sent among you. And ye shall eat in plenty, and be satisfied, and praise the name of the LORD your God, that hath dealt wondrously with you: and my people shall never be ashamed."

Stand in faith for your family. Don't let the day-to-day pink pigs distract you and miss what God is saying and doing in this new era. The desire of our Heavenly Father is that families are united as one in His love. So, let's not allow ourselves to become fatigued or distracted. God, working through our prayers, will take action in the lives of our children.

> At the right time, we will harvest a good crop if we don't give up or quit.
>
> Galatians 6:9, MSG

NOTE:
Country music legend, Ricky Skaggs is a product of a Praying Mama. Skaggs is modest about his achievements, feeling that he is simply God's instrument. In his concerts, Ricky often sings, "I Heard My Mother Call My Name In Prayer," acknowledging the power of a Praying Mother. Ricky Skaggs was inducted into the Country Music Hall of Fame in 2018.

> "I Heard My Mother Call My Name in Prayer"
> While kneeling by her bedside in a cottage on the hill
> My mother prayed her blessings on me there
> She was talking there to Jesus while everything was still
> And I heard my mother call my name in prayer

Yes, I heard my mother call my name in prayer
She was pourin' out her heart to Jesus there
Then I gave my heart to Him and He saved my soul
from sin
For He heard my mother call my name in prayer

She was anxious for her boy to be just what he ought
to be
And she asked the Lord to take him in His care
Just the words I can't remember but I know she
prayed for me
For I heard my mother call my name in prayer

So I gave my heart to Jesus and I'm livin' now for
Him
And someday I'll go and meet Him in the air
For He heard my mother praying and He saved my
soul from sin
Yes, He heard my mother call my name in prayer [1]

[1] *I Heard My Mother Call My Name In Prayer*. Lyrics by written by Harry F. Chapin, Sandy Chapin. Lyrics licensed by LyricFind.

סֶלָה

SELAH
PAUSE—PONDER—PRAY

PAUSE

> The power of God comes like a mighty
> locomotive. The rails it travels on are our
> prayers. We were created to have conversations
> with God.[1]
>
> — Watchman Nee

PONDER

Earth is depending on you to pray. The families on Earth are
depending on you to pray. Your children and children's children
are depending on you to pray. All creation is depending on you
to pray. Heaven is depending on you to pray; the list goes on.

Even though much of your focus is on all of the above,
and rightly so; however, you must not forget to pray for yourself
as well. You have been entrusted to intercede and not get
distracted. You may find yourself in need of God's perspective
and wisdom more than ever before in order to fulfill your
obligation to your generation and to the future of planet Earth.

PRAYER

Father, thank You that You've entrusted me to pray for my
generation. Grant me the grace to be faithful to pray for them
and to never get too busy to come to You with their needs and
my needs. I pray for the wisdom to know what's most important
in this season and for Your love to cover all I say and do.
I pray this in Jesus' Name. Amen!

---

[1] **https://quotesthoughtsrandom.wordpress.com/2015/06/30/how-does-gods-power-come-to-us**. Accessed 03/28/2019.

CHAPTER 8

Where Is Your Apron?

Praying Mama: Susanna Wesley

Susanna's place in Christian history is indeed based on what her sons accomplished, but it could be said it was her example and influence that helped them to do what they did. Susanna's best legacy was her children. Susanna never preached a sermon or published a book or founded a church, yet, is known as the Mother of Methodism.

— Mother of Charles and John Wesley

> Here's what I want you to do: Find a quiet, secluded place: Just be there as simply and honestly as you can manage. The focus will shift from you to God, you will begin to sense his grace.
>
> Matthew 6:6, MSG, paraphrase mine

I was nonchalantly listening as the airline flight attendant gave the customary safety instructions. This was not my first time to fly so the briefing was not new to me. For some reason, the part concerning the possibility of cabin decompression caught my attention. She went through the rhetoric of what to do in the event there was a sudden drop in cabin pressure and how to secure the oxygen mask over our nose and mouth. The following directive is what caught my attention: "If you are traveling with a small child, secure your mask on first, then assist your child."

My immediate thought was I had misunderstood the instructions. A responsible parent would never attend to their personal safety first and leave their child in a vulnerable situation. The instructions kept nagging at me until I realized the Lord was trying to teach me a spiritual lesson using the analogy of airline safety. To lend credence to the warning, I decided to ask a friend of mine, an airline flight attendant, about the directive. She unequivocally answered my question with the following statement, "You would not believe the disasters we've faced because passengers, refused to heed the airline's survival instructions, *take care of themselves first before attending the need of their child.*" She reiterated it again, "In an emergency situation, it is imperative that caregivers (in this case we're talking about mothers) must first attend to their personal safety in order to insure the welfare of their children."

What a spiritual analogy this is for Praying Mamas, those who are called to intercede for this radical, world-changing generation, and the crisis they face daily.

Praying Mamas, if you stop and look at yourselves, you will see a group of mind-blowing human beings. For nine months, you carried within your body, fed, protected and eventually delivered a human being with an eternal soul. You are so impassioned with the successfulness of your family, you often set aside your own gifts and desires in order to help them succeed.

As a mother, you are most likely the one who confronts and conquers the war zone of the home. Daily, without warning, you experience a world of overwhelming and ever-changing demands. You are often the more present and available parent as your children quickly become young men and women. Through adoption, many of you welcome sons and daughters into your home and heart, whom you didn't get to welcome into the world through birth. If necessary, without doubt, you would lay your life down for one of your children; as a mother, that's the way you're wired.

As the wife of a minister and a mother, more often than not, I had to ruminate on Isaiah 40:29-31 just to make it through a day. A visiting minister once prayed over me and said, "I see you going up a slide backward, on the slippery side, struggling to get to the top so you can slide down like everyone else." Little did he know that depicted me trying to do all that was expected of me as a mother and wife of a pastor.

> God strengthens the weary and gives vitality to those worn down by age and care. Young people will get tired; strapping young men will stumble and fall. But those who trust in (wait on) the Eternal One will regain their strength. They will soar on wings as eagles. They will run — never winded, never weary. They will walk — never tired, never faint.
> Isaiah 40:29-31 The Voice Bible [1]

In his book, *Kentucky Traveler,* Ricky Skaggs wrote about a mother.

> Mothers are the soul of a family, and they model the faith in a way that nobody else can. I'm convinced there is no way two men can do the work of one woman.[2]

To successfully deal with the pressures of motherhood and the crisis of future generations, we must first secure our spiritual strength by waiting daily in the presence of Jesus. If we want to be victorious in attending both the spiritual and the natural welfare of our children, taking care of our spiritual well-being is unavoidable. Daily, we must make a conscientious effort to find our own place in order renew our strength.

Paul admonished Timothy, "Take heed unto thyself" (1 Timothy 4:16, NKJV). As a mother, it is so easy to become

---

[1] The Voice Bible, eBook, Thomas Nelson, Kindle Edition, p. 839.
[2] Ricky Skaggs, *Kentucky Traveler,* p.317.

distracted by things that call out for your attention. Let me give you a word of caution: If your relationship with God suffers because you are trying to meet the needs of everyone else, it will be just a matter of time until you run dry, lose your energy and passion, and have nothing more to give.

As an intercessor in God's end-time army, you must set aside some private time to develop your own relationship with God. It is imperative that you don't neglect your own spiritual needs and be refreshed by the Word. You can only give what you have inside. Paul warned Timothy, "Don't get so busy that you forget your own spiritual needs." I like to think that if Paul was writing this book to encourage you as intercessors, he might have said it like this:

> Praying Mama, get ahold of yourself. Make your own spiritual life a priority. Don't get so busy that you forget that you have spiritual needs too.

I've always made an attempt to have my time with the Lord. It was a necessary habit of mine. Your time of prayer will become a spiritual addiction that your body, soul and spirit crave. Nothing can satisfy that power or desire other than time alone in the presence of Jesus. In his book, *The Secret of The Stairs*, Wade Taylor wrote:

> By divine intention, it is not possible for us to find spiritual satisfaction or fulfillment in anything less than developing a love relationship with Jesus.[1]

We all have heard the old adage, "It's easier said than done." I promise you, finding time to sit in the Presence of Jesus can be done. Our Heavenly Father sees all, hears all, and knows all. He

---

[1] Taylor E. Wade, *The Secret of The Stairs*; Advanced Global Publishing, Kindle Locations, p. 477-479.

understands the load you carry as mothers. Do not allow condemnation to be your constant companion if you can't spend hours in prayer like some you may know or have read about. Adopt the Nike® slogan, Just Do It, which was coined from the phrase, Let's Do It.

One of my favorite Praying Mamas is Susanna Wesley, a busy mama with a dysfunctional family. When Susanna was young, she promised the Lord that for every hour she spent in entertainment, she would give to Him in prayer and in the Word. Taking care of the house and raising so many children made this commitment almost impossible to fulfill. She had no time for entertainment or long hours in prayer! She worked the gardens, milked the cow, schooled the children, and managed the entire house herself. She decided instead to give the Lord two hours a day in prayer! She struggled to find a secret place to get away with Him so she advised her children that when they saw her with her apron over her head, it meant she was in prayer and couldn't be disturbed. She was devoted to her walk with Christ, praying for her children, and knowledge in the Word, no matter how hard life was.

Susanna had a strong prayer life and believed in daily prayer, but behind the door of her home, hopeless conditions were the norm. She was married to a preacher; a man who couldn't manage money. They disagreed on everything from money to politics. They had 19 children in 21 years. All except ten died in infancy. Sam, her husband, left her to raise the children alone for long periods of time. This was sometimes over something as simple as an argument. Going through the maze of her life, we can easily recognize her number one priority was her walk with Christ, devotion to the Word of God, and praying for her children.

Praying Mamas, if sitting in His presence is new to you, don't feel bad, Just Do It. For starters, I challenge you to set aside 15 minutes a day to be shut in with God in that secret place of His presence in order to gain new strength to successfully war for your family, community, and nation. You will be pleasantly surprised when your prayer time evolves into a time of gratification each time you symbolically pull your apron over your head to have your time of spiritual renewing. There is nothing as gratifying as time spent in your secret place under the Shadow of the Almighty.

I encourage you to memorize Psalm 91. Declare it daily over yourself and your family. This Psalm is known as the Psalm of protection and deliverance for those who habitually dwell in the secret place, desiring an intimate relationship with the Almighty. "He that dwelleth in the secret place of the most High shall abide under the shadow of the Almighty" (Psalm 91:1).

In the hurriedness of life, it is God's plan that we gather in the shelter of His dwelling to find rest under His shadow. His gift to mothers is long-term rest and refuge in His place of dwelling. It's available to all of us, but all do not choose to dwell in that shelter.

Charles Spurgeon, the great English preacher of the 19th century, said, "They run to it at times, and enjoy occasional approaches, but they do not habitually reside in the mysterious presence."[1]

Here are a few safety tips that might help you as you embark upon your spiritual journey of your secret place dwelling. Find time daily to be alone with God in a quiet, secluded place where you won't be disturbed. This time usually includes thanksgiving, praise, and worship. There will be days when you will desire your worship music, other times you will want to just sit quietly, soaking in His Presence. Allow time for introspection and meditation. This can be extremely valuable in developing your quiet time. Spend time reading a portion of the scriptures. God often speaks through a verse you have hidden away in memory, or one you have just read. Practice being still, He tells us, "Be still and know that I am God."

There are no set rules in developing your daily time alone with God. Be careful not to get into legalism about your prayer

---

[1] C.H. Spurgeon, *The Treasury of David*, Volume 2, Peabody, MA: Hendrickson Publishers.

time. Don't be haunted with fear that something drastic might happen if you don't spend a specific amount of time on your knees or miss that time altogether. I have been there and done that. I assure you, God's grace is big enough to keep your family if you occasionally miss your prayer time. Just enjoy your time alone with the Almighty and the peace He gives, "that passes all understanding." I have learned one thing for certain, the enemy of our soul, the deceiver, cannot duplicate this God-given peace.

We can be the best mom, wife, friend, person in the world and still have untold hardships. We need to take Susanna's example, flip our apron over our head and pray in the middle of it all. Hidden behind the door of our homes, I want our children to see PRAYING MAMAS who pray diligently no matter how busy or how hard the circumstances.

In September 2015, prophetess Lana Vawser shared a prophetic vision God gave her concerning mothers. The following is a segment of that vision concerning a personal breakthrough for you:

> In this vision, Jesus approached these mothers one by one, and with such tenderness and love, He caressed their cheeks and spoke, "I have heard your cries, I have heard your prayers and great breakthrough is before you. As you have positioned yourself before Me with a heart of hunger and surrender, I am meeting with you. I am taking you into depths you have never known. In these deep places of intimacy, you will be strengthened, you will be refreshed and much will be restored to you, as you press into Me and allow My Spirit to lead you into deeper realms and encounters.
>
> You will no longer feel like you are running on empty. You will no longer feel you are scraping from the bottom of the barrel. Where you have felt you have been stretched for time, I will

release double to you in shorter amounts of time. I am going to meet with many of you in prophetic dreams and much will be released to you. You will begin to feel you are living out of the overflow that is found in Me, than out of just enough. A shift is taking place over you!"[1]

NOTE:
Who are John and Charles Wesley? John and Charles Wesley did not set out to establish a church, but the Wesleyans and the Methodists are their offspring. Both preached, and wrote hymns. John is more noted for his sermons and Charles for his hymns. John said this about his mother, "I learned more about Christianity from my mother than from all the theologians in England."

[1] Lana Vawser, **https://lanavawser.com/2015/09/03/mothers-are-arising**. Accessed 3/28/2019.

סֶלָה

SELAH
PAUSE–PONDER–PRAY

Prayer has in it the possibility to affect everything
that affects us.[1]

— E. M. Bounds

PAUSE

Don't fret or worry. Instead of worrying, pray.
Let petitions and praises shape your worries into
prayers, letting God know your concerns.

Philippians 4:6, MSG

PONDER

Distraction is, always has been, and probably always will be,
inherent in a woman's life.

- What hindrances keep you from praying?
- How would you have to view God in order to come
  to Him with expectation and trust when you pray?
- How will you deal with distractions?

Consider writing your responses to these questions.

PRAY

Let the father know your worries and concerns.

1 Peter 5:1

Father in Jesus' Name, I thank You that You are always thinking
about me and watching everything that concerns me, and that

---

[1] www.fbbc.com/messages/bounds_possibilities_c09.htm. Accessed
March 2, 2019.

You want me to give You my worries and cares. Here's what I'm burdened about today.

Lord, life is so busy, and I have a hard time being still. Thank You that You receive me where I am today and that I can cast all my cares upon You.

I pray this in Jesus' Name. Amen!

CHAPTER 9

The Power Of Blessing

Praying Mama: Mary Ball Washington

Mary Ball Washington was a somewhat nervous and overprotective mother. Before her son left for a war that his mother begged him not to engage in, it is said that he knelt before his mother's rocking chair while she prayed for God's protection on his life. Washington later credited his mother's prayers for his surviving many crises and several massacres in the British campaigns that followed.[1]

— Mary Ball Washington, the Mother of George Washington,
First President of the United States

> O God, You have taught me from my youth; and to this day I declare Your wondrous works. Now also when I am old and gray headed, O God, do not forsake me, until I declare Your strength to this generation, Your power to everyone who is to come.
>
> Psalm 71:17-18, AMP

Hearing the patriarch of our family confer blessings upon his children is how it all started with me. We had a large clan, and from an early age we were taught to respect the patriarch and matriarch of our tribe. We called them Grannie and Grandpa. We often gathered at their home to enjoy family, fun, and fellowship. Without fail, as the gathering came to an end, we

---

[1] George Washington **https://nccs.net/products/the-bulletproof-george-washington**. Accessed April 1, 2019.

convened in the living room in front of their big stone fireplace to be blessed by Grandpa, the elder statesman of our family.

To this day, I still remember how my grandparents blessed each family before they embarked upon their journey home. Hearing someone call your name in prayer will make an imprint on your soul. We were a rather large group, but Grannie and Grandpa never stopped until each of the children and their families were called by name. Bestowing blessings was not an occasional happening, it was every time they had a guest in their home, including family or friends. If there is one thing I learned from those gatherings, it is that "An impartation of supernatural power accompanies the concept of speaking blessings over our tribe."

As mothers, we are within our comfort zone with the concept of interceding for our families, but the theory of speaking blessings over families is a lost or foreign theology to us. The purpose of this chapter is to encourage you to start the practice of speaking blessings over your children and grandchildren. God had a reason for instituting the concept of blessing. He planned for life to be imparted to His children through the spoken blessing. You can read about the conveyance of blessings throughout scripture.

God used the spoken blessing personally to impart favor to His people. He verbally blessed Adam and Eve (Genesis 1:28), Abraham (Genesis 12:1-3), and Jacob (Genesis 32:24-32). Jesus spoke blessings over the lives of His disciples (Matthew 5:1-16). Throughout the Bible, blessings are spoken over the people of God. It is the duty of parents to follow the established plan of the patriarchs to insure the success of blessing upon their children.

Praying Mama, you were created to be God's agent of blessing to your children not an agent of cursing. Blessing children on a regular basis is a necessary practice which aids in the fulfillment of the identities and destinies of future generations.

Blessing is God's primary mechanism of imparting His image into the deep places of a person's heart including their thoughts, feelings and experience regarding identity, such as *Who am I?*, and into their destiny, such as *Why am I here?*. This is critically important because vision for life, physical and emotional health, financial prosperity, and family relational dynamics are all directly linked to images of God, self, and others imprinted in the inner man, the soul, of every person (3 John 2).[1]

No wonder the enemy of our souls, Satan, does not want us to affirm our children. He wants you to feel awkward when you speak blessings out loud. He understands the power in releasing those blessings. Jack Hayford says this about blessing our children:

> To shape a child for tomorrow is to shape tomorrow's world, and to shape a child in God's wholesome order of blessing is to multiply the same to that child's entire realm of future influence. It is the same thing as bequeathing an inheritance to the next generation.[2]

I enjoy studying Jewish history. Several years ago, a Jewish friend gave me a book entitled *Jewish Literacy* by Rabbi Joseph Telushkin. It is an analysis of the most important things to know about the Jewish religion, its people, and its history.

The Jewish culture understands the importance of blessing their children. Traditionally, Jewish families gather together each week on Friday evening, Erev Shabbat in Hebrew, for a special meal and a pronouncement of blessing. I won't go into all the ceremonial details of Shabbat; however, it is vital for us to understand at this time each week, the Jewish father prays

---

[1] Craig Hill, The Power of a Parent's Blessing: See Your Children Prosper and Fulfill Their Destinies in Christ, Charisma House. Kindle Edition, p. 10.

[2] Jack Hayford, Blessing Your Children: Baker Publishing Group, 2012, 22-23.

a blessing over his wife and then pronounces a blessing over each of his children. In many Jewish families, the father also proclaims vision and prosperity over his children thus, creating in his offspring an expectation of future success.

Some of you may be thinking, *I am a single mom, what am I to do?* or perhaps *My husband is not a Christian; therefore, my children will miss out on receiving a blessing.* You older moms and grandmas need to understand that it's not too late for you to speak blessings over your family. All of those are lies of the enemy. Rabbi Telushkin wrote, "The father customarily blesses the children, but mothers can do so as well." He puts his hands over each child's head saying to the boys, "May God make you like Ephraim and Menashe (Manasseh)." (the two sons of Joseph.) When he blesses the girls, he says, "May God make you like Sarah, Rebecca, and Leah" (the Matriarchs).[1]

I believe it is God's intent for every child, no matter their ethnicity, to grow up in a culture of blessing. You may not fully understand the phrase, "a culture of blessing." Simply stated, "It is an environment in which family members regularly convey to one another God's message of value rather than Satan's message of worthlessness."

God does not push, nor does He shove. He won't force us, He does not violate our right to choose. He gives us free will and opportunities to speak blessings over our children and the next generation. The principle of blessing is based on two scriptures:

> Death and life are in the power of the tongue,
> and those who love it will eat its fruit.
> Proverbs 18:21, NKJV

---

[1] Rabbi Joseph Telushkin, *Jewish Literacy, Sabbath Rituals In The House*, William Morrow and Company, 1991, p. 321, 675.

Not returning evil for evil or reviling for reviling,
but on the contrary bless, knowing that you were
called to this, that you may inherit a blessing.
1 Peter 3:9, NKJV

I will say this without doubt, family blessing or cursing, speaking
life or death to our children, will more often than not influence
the course of a child's destiny, not for just one generation, but
for many generations to come. Just one word, whether ill spoken
or perfectly timed, can leave an imprint on a child's soul.[1]

Both blessing and cursing are seeds that will reproduce
after their kind for generations. Kind words will produce warmth
and build relationships but harsh words breed tension, anxiety
and separation. The fact is, words are powerful and are most
important in developing meaningful relationships in our families,
friends, communities, and our nation.

While expounding on the truths of this chapter, I want
to share an example that lends credibility to the theory of how
the atmosphere of a home affects children. Recently, while
attending a softball tournament, I overheard a conversation at
the concession stand that dumbfounded me. While waiting for
my food, I heard some of the lewdest jargon and cursing I have
ever heard. I quickly turned to see who had the nerve to speak
such language in public. To my surprise it was two young boys
the approximate age of my great grandsons. They may have been
grade school level, but what was coming out of their mouth was
verbiage most adults would hesitate to use. I felt as if someone
hit me square in the gut. My first impulse was to correct them,
but I restrained myself when I noticed several adults around me
who seemed to be unscathed by the two young boys and their
offensive behavior. For the rest of the game, I rehearsed the
incident in my mind. I pondered, What if what I heard coming
from the mouth of those two young boys was the product of

---

[1] Jack Hayford, *Blessing Your Children*, Baker Publishing Group, Regal
House Publishing, Raleigh, NC, 2002, p. 96..

their parents speaking death and vulgarity around their precious seed, the results reproducing after their kind for generations to come.

Praying Mamas, you can change this pattern and leave a new legacy for future generations by creating a family culture of blessing. The greatest gift you can leave for the next generation is the practice of blessing your children. We, as parents, should accept our responsibility to create a culture of blessing in our homes and reproduce this culture within our communities. If we don't, the results affect many children, hindering them from prospering and fulfilling their destinies.

The concept of blessing our children is very clear. God has given parents the privilege and power to speak blessings upon their children. It is interesting to note, even Jesus needed His father's blessing. Jesus Himself did not perform one miracle nor preach one sermon until after He had publicly received the blessing of His Father. That is a prime example of how important blessing our children is. The Gospel of Luke depicts the Father's words as He blessed His Son, Jesus.

> The Holy Spirit descended upon Him in bodily form like a dove, and a voice came out of heaven, "You are My beloved Son, in You I am well pleased."
>
> Luke 3:22

I am convinced this blessing from His heavenly Father is what gave Jesus the needed strength to walk in His true identity and fulfill His destiny on Earth. If Jesus needed the blessing of His Father in order to complete His destiny, so do our children need to receive a similar blessing to walk in their true identity and destiny.

We live in a crazed society where our children go to school, facing the possibility of some deranged individual walking into their classroom with a semi-automatic weapon and releasing a barrage of bullets upon their teachers, friends, and possibly themselves, dying in their own pool of blood.

Our children should never feel the effects of gun violence in their school. We, as Praying Mamas, are commissioned by God Himself to rescue children from the horrible, murderous pit the enemy has planned. The privilege of speaking blessings over our children is another powerful feature of raising our children, protecting them in every way we can. Never forget, you are God's Manifesto, and part of His end-time army.

In order to establish a culture of blessing in our home, we need to follow some simple principles:

1. **Speak Blessings Often!**
    Have regular times when you lay your hands upon your child's head, gently; sometimes even quietly while they sleep. The power of spoken blessings is an excellent way to establish a culture of blessing in your home. Our words have great influence in the lives of those around us. Spoken blessings can bring hope, encouragement, and direction to our families. When you speak blessings upon your children, you direct God's goodness to them. I have included a copy of Psalm 91 in this book to declare over them daily.

2. **Use a Biblical Framework for Blessings!**
    The priestly blessing, recorded in Numbers, provides us with an excellent example of a Godly blessing.

    The Lord bless thee, and keep [guard, protect, compass about with a hedge of safety] thee: The Lord make his face shine upon thee, and be gracious unto thee: The Lord lift up his countenance [give full attention in a favorable way] upon thee, and give thee peace [wholeness, health, security, serenity, well-being, contentment, harmony; an absence of negative stress, disturbance, tension, and conflict].
    Numbers 6:24-26, AMP

You can use this blessing as a framework for composing blessings. Speak or even whisper the words of this blessing, knowing that you are anointed by the living God to declare and decree blessings upon your family. God Himself will attend to the Word spoken because it is His Word you are speaking and it's according to His will.

Jesus Himself provided a prime example of how to bless our children. When several parents brought their children to Him, He took them up in His arms, laid His hands on them and blessed them (Mark 10:1).

I believe it is significantly important, whenever possible, touch your children as you impart your words of blessing. They will experience the feeling of satisfaction that you are focusing your attention on them as you touch and speak blessing upon them. Yes, you will feel awkward at first, but it is well worth the effort of pushing through. God Himself has given you that privilege and the authority to do so.

3. **Forming a habit of blessing is appropriate!**
   You may want to be creative in the way you bestow blessings upon your child. No rules or requirements are needed as you confer blessings upon your children. They just need to hear the affirming voice of their mother or father. (As you speak these words in prayer or speak them directly to the person for whom they are written, you will invoke the power, grace, and blessings of God upon them.)

Also, you could write out the blessing and use it as a great source of encouragement in your child's life and create a culture of blessing in your home.

In order to attain a diversity in conferring blessings, you may want to consider using the various Names of God, asking Him to apply the power that each name represents; thus, applying it to the need of your child. For years I have carried a list of the Names of God using them in my prayer guide for my family.

I have listed below the most commonly referenced Names of God. Each name represents a different aspect of His character and a suggestion of how to use the name:

Jehovah-Jireh
The Lord Our Provider, Genesis 22:14
Speak a blessing in the face of specific need, whatever realm the need may represent.

Jehovah-Raah
The Lord Our Shepherd, Psalm 23:1
Speak a blessing with the reminder of God's never-forsaking presence and protection.

Jehovah-Shalom
The Lord Our Peace, Judges 6:24
Speak a blessing that will comfort in the midst of turmoil or upset.

Jehovah-Rapha
The Lord Our Healer, Exodus 15:26
Speak a blessing that calls for God's grace of healing, knowing that He wants to heal the sick.[1]

Praying Mama, through faith in the blood of Jesus, you have spiritual authority over your household. We need to fully understand we have the ability to influence both in our personal life, our family, and the future of our nation through the powerful act of speaking blessings.

I recommend writing out scriptures or even the blessings you will speak over your family. These imprints upon your heart

---

[1] Larry Lea, *Could You Not Tarry One Hour?* (Lake Mary, FL: Creation House, 1987

encourage you to execute them in your actions. Speaking blessings is the foundation stone for successful family and community.

Satan sees our children as the greatest threat to his plans. He will do anything he can to prevent parents from imparting life into their children through spoken blessing.

Praying Mama, your voiceprint can leave a lasting imprint on your child's soul. There is a generation of children all around us, and God wants us to take care of them.

סֶלָה

SELAH
PAUSE–PONDER–PRAY

PAUSE

Accomplishing the ministry of blessing our seed requires two things. We must answer the call with confidence believing that blessing our children is an assignment from God Himself.

PONDER

Dwight L. Moody returned from an evangelistic service at a local church one evening. A friend asked, "Reverend Moody, were there any converts tonight?" The renowned evangelist paused a moment, enumerating the results, and replied, "Yes, there were three and one-half." To this, the friend responded, "Ah, three adults and a child." But Moody replied, "No, there were three children and an adult." He then continued, answering the bewildered look on the inquirer's face, "An adult only has half a life remaining to live for Christ, but the children will have the entirety of their lives to know His blessing and serve His will."[1]

PRAY

Father, let my hands become instruments of Your blessings. Lord, what I plant in my children through the impartation of Your blessings, let it grow until it becomes a part of them.

Father, fill me daily with Your Holy Spirit, and keep my soul overflowing with Your wisdom and goodness. Lord, I speak blessings and affirmation toward my children so they may become godly parents and leaders of tomorrow.

I pray this in Jesus' Name. Amen!

---

[1] Jack Hayford. *Blessing your Child*, Regal House Publishing, Raleigh, NC, 2002, p.110.

CHAPTER 10

Let Your Voice Be Heard

Praying Mama: Monica of Hippo

Monica's closing years were filled with joy at seeing the great powers of her son, wholly given to the service of God. His writings are a constant testimony to her character. In his confessions, Augustine spoke of his grief and weeping for his mother, recognizing her part in his salvation. In his later years, Augustine could look back on his life and recognize the importance of his mother's perseverance in prayer in winning him to the Christian faith. Even when things looked their darkest, Monica never quit praying for the salvation of her family. She persevered in prayer, trusting God with the outcome, and saw the ones she loved brought into the family of God.

— Mother of St. Augustine

> Stand up and yell in the night with all your heart; call to God even while the city sleeps during the night watch; Pour out your heart like water in the presence of the Lord! Lift your hands and plead to Him for the lives of your children.
> Lamentation 2:19, The Voice Bible

Have you ever whined to God? If you haven't, you're a much more mature daughter than I am. In the early days of our ministry, I thought having a name known in religious circles was the ultimate goal of every minister. Relatively speaking, my husband and I successfully served as pastors of several churches, missionaries to Indonesia, and in any capacity God asked us to serve. However, the enemy convinced me that I was just a minister's wife with a No Name Ministry. I often complained to God, reminding Him of friends who were called upon to be conference speakers and often featured on popular religious magazines and TV shows. I would not have appeared on a TV show if asked, I just wanted a name. I believe that's called pride. I was consistently on a spiritual pity party. Aren't you glad He is a merciful God who doesn't send fire down from Heaven when we grumble and complain?

One morning during one of my bouts of whining, Holy Spirit asked me the following question, and I will ask you the same question, "Would you rather your name be known by man, or would you rather have your name be known in Heaven and in hell?" Of course, we all agree, we want our names known in Heaven.

When we consider how each of us is unique, you might initially think of things like your looks or your fingerprints. However, you have a voiceprint which identifies you as uniquely as your DNA, fingerprints or physical features. Your voiceprint is what identifies you as the person speaking, the same as your fingerprints identify you as the person you are. Voiceprints are used in voice ID systems for user authentication. Some people might sound quite a bit alike, but no two voices ever sound exactly the same. That is the uniqueness of God, and how He created each of us to have a one-of-a-kind voice.

Isn't it humbling to think that God, in His eternal plan, created us and gave us our own unique voiceprint to be His Voice on Earth, generating enough power to activate His Word? God's full intention is that we are to be vocal when we are in combat with the enemy of our soul. Our voice becomes a weapon of mass destruction against the enemy when we vocally declare and decree God's Word over our families and the occurrences we face daily.

When we activate God's Word based upon the finished work of Calvary, both Heaven and hell recognize our voice, announcing that we are advancing in war for the lives of our children, our community, and our nation. When we declare God's Word, the Holy Spirit alerts warring angels that are assigned to assist us both in the heavenly and in earth realms.

The Holy Spirit does not have to announce to the demonic forces of hell that you are using your voice as a weapon of war. They hear every word you say, and it causes them to shrink back in fear, knowing Jesus has stripped them of their authority and has given it to you to rule Earth for Kingdom purposes. The war over who has dominion on Earth started when Satan was kicked out of Heaven.

As intercessors and warriors, we must have an understanding about the magnitude of having our names known in hell. If we have a relationship with Jesus and truly understand the authority we have in His Name then our name and our voiceprint is known in hell and becomes a constant threat to the enemy of our soul, Satan himself. The enemy's power is diminished the moment we speak the Word of God, using our voice as a weapon of war. When our feet hit the floor each morning, demonic forces should tremble at the thought that you, as a warrior, are up and ready for battle.

Praying Mama, it is Jesus in you that gives you the power to use your voice as a weapon. This kind of authority is born out of an intimate relationship and daily communication with Him. The more you know Him, the more Spiritual Authority you have.

> Jesus said, "My sheep hear My voice, and I know them, (I recognize their voice) and they follow Me."
> John 10:27, KJV

As we hear the voice of God, and wholly follow Him, then and only then can our voiceprint become a weapon of war. In the natural, if we spend time with an individual and have a relationship with them, we will readily recognize their voice in a venue of many voices. It is difficult to comprehend that in the midst of millions of warring mamas, God can readily distinguish each individual voice as they cry out to Him in their times of woe. If He knows when you lose one hair from your head, He can without a doubt hear your voice when you cry out to Him.

Years ago I read and have kept in my reference file what Reinhart Bonnke had to say about the Holy Spirit and the Word. He addressed it simply and to the point, "We have to voice the Word in order to put it into action. God is counting on your voice. Without our words, He has nothing to work with."

The Holy Spirit is the One that associates so closely with us; He baptizes us. He operates only through the Word of God. Until the Word is spoken, He does nothing. Look at creation, where He hovered like a wind over the face of chaos. When God said, "Let there be Light," He brought Light. That is why we need Holy Spirit preaching, the Spirit blesses the Word. No one else can do that. By Him, the Word of God becomes a life-giving, life-changing power. Nobody can preach with Holy Spirit power unless we preach the Word of God. He is committed to the Word and the living link between God and the Word. That is His eternal association. The Spirit acts when the Word is spoken.

Holy Spirit told me, "My word in your mouth is just as powerful as My Word in My mouth." The power is in the Word of God.

Praying Mamas, your voiceprint, your voice, is a weapon that causes hell to tremble when you cry out to God on behalf of your family, community and nation. When we use our voice to speak God's Word over our circumstances, things have to change. His Word will not return void.

> So shall my word be that goeth forth out of my mouth: it shall not return unto me void, but it shall accomplish that which I please, and it shall prosper in the thing whereto I sent it.
>
> Isaiah 55:11, KJV

Years ago I heard the following statement which I believe is so true, "The word works for those who work the word."

If we want things to change, it is crucial that we use our voice to inflict harm on the enemy of our soul. You need to read the whole of Daniel, chapter ten. I would like to call attention to Daniel 10:12:

> He said unto me, "Fear not, Daniel: for from the first day that thou didst set thine heart to understand, and to chasten thyself before thy God, Thy Words were heard, and I am come for Thy Words."

The angel Gabriel was sent to encourage Daniel during the time of intense warfare. His first words to Daniel were *Fear not.* In the battle over our families, we must first conquer the voice of fear and intimidation. That is one of the weapons in the devil's collection of military equipment.

Notice, the messenger of God did not say, "Daniel, I have come because you are a highly respected man and highly regarded by God. His words were, "Thy *words* were heard, and I am come because of your *words.*" Daniel's voiceprint identified him in the battle over the destiny of his people.

More often than not, when we declare God's Word in battle, the enemy will try everything in his arsenal to challenge you and thwart your victory. Another weapon he tries to use is doubt. He may whisper to your thoughts: *God does not hear you, look at your past* or *the Word may work for some, but it doesn't work for you.* Daniel was assured that his voice was heard the first day he called out. The messenger, Gabriel, gave Daniel an explanation in verse 13 of why he was delayed in his coming, "I would have been here sooner; however, for the past 21 days the spirit prince of Persia, demonic antagonism, opposed me and prevented my coming to you. Then Michael, one of the chief princes of Heaven, came to my aid because I alone was busy dealing with the kings of Persia" (The Voice Bible).

We should pray the following scripture every day and never give up on our children. We must persevere and wait with expectancy regardless of circumstances:

> Listen to my *voice* in the morning, Lord. Each morning I bring my requests to you and *wait expectantly*.
>
> Psalm 5:3, NLT, (emphasis mine)

Daniel waited expectantly even though things didn't change right away. He persevered regardless of his circumstances.

Praying Mamas, it's not easy to stand our ground when the odds are against us. This little idiomatic expression paints a perfect picture of continuing even in the face of difficulties: *By perseverance the snail reached the ark*.

The story in Daniel, chapter ten, should encourage us to use our voice as a weapon to war on behalf of this millennial generation and situations that surround them. God is no respecter of persons. If He sent help because of Daniel's words, He will also harken unto your words. Never fear, *help is on the way*. God will send you someone or something to aid you in the war that you are engaged in. It may be in the form of an angel, a friend to join with you in agreement, or a word directly from God's Word. Rest assured, He will send you help.

Daily we should proclaim, *Give me this mountain*. We must take back the Family Mountain if we want to establish a culture of blessing in our homes and communities.

I call Acts 2 the Power chapter. All Christian religious groups recognize the Day of Pentecost as the day the Holy Spirit fell on the Early Church in the Upper Room. Ordinary people were empowered to use their voice to proclaim God's Word. I don't think it was just happenstance. God used the illustration of *tongues of fire* to imprint on our soul the fact that He wants His Church, you and me, to be a vocal church. The reason He gave each of us a unique voiceprint is so we can be easily identified in both Heaven and hell when we use our voice to speak the oracles of God. He has given us an anointed voice to speak. That is the reason our enemy, Satan, is so desperate to shut down our voice. God responds to the voice of His daughters, His End-time Manifesto.

Can you imagine what it must have been like in the Upper Room when the sound came? Suddenly, without warning, sounds roar from the sky, and the whole room reverberates with the sound of violent wind. Then tongues of fire landed on the heads of all those present, baptizing them with the Holy Spirit.

To the disciples present, the sound was a sound of *victory*. To those in the city, I am sure it was a sound of *amazement*. To the devil and all his cohorts, I am sure it was the sound of *war*! Praying Mamas, use your voice as a weapon. Don't remain silent! God wants you to be a vocal warrior. Your voice is a Sound of War to the enemy of our soul.

As I close this chapter, I would like to share with you a portion of a prophetic word over mothers:

Breakthrough For Children

> The Lord is honoring the prayers of mothers. Many have been crying many tears over their children. Many have felt like they have come to a place where they don't know what to do anymore. In this season as the mothers continue to press in, I saw the Lord releasing *strategy* to mothers for their children that are going to bring specific, long-awaited breakthrough into their lives. I saw children being healed in the multitudes. Freedom was coming to their children, from young children to adults. Freedom and healing were exploding all around. Sudden turnaround miracles were occurring as these mothers implemented the strategies of Heaven, strategies of His heart and *miracles* were beginning to take place in huge, unexpected ways. I felt the Lord's heart of encouragement for mothers to not give up. Do not give up

praying for your children. The Lord is honoring your prayers, and a point of breakthrough for mothers is right now as they keep standing. Prodigals are returning home in multitudes.[1]

I declare this word over you and encourage you to use your voice to destroy the enemy's hold over your children and grandchildren.

NOTE:

Saint Augustine of Hippo (/ɔː ˈɡʌstɪn/; 13 November 354 – 28 August 430 AD) was a Roman African, early Christian theologian and philosopher from Numidia whose writings influenced the development of Western Christianity and Western philosophy. He was the bishop of Hippo Regius in North Africa and is viewed as one of the most important Church Fathers in Western Christianity for his writings in the Patristic Period. Among his most important works are The City of God, On Christian Doctrine and Confessions.[2]

---

[1] Lana Vawser, *Mothers Are Arising!* September 3, 2015.

[2] https://en.wikipedia.org/wiki/Augustine_of_Hippo.

סֶלָה

SELAH
PAUSE–PONDER–PRAY

PAUSE

If you want to change this generation *and* the complexion of our culture, be your very best in the darkest moments. *You can, you will, you must!*

PONDER

God is preparing Praying Mamas to be His confident and bold warriors.

You must rise above your fears, doubts and fatigue. No matter how dark it gets, you must complete the assignment God has given you. This is what separates you from everyone else. Meditate on the following scripture.

> The Eternal is with me, so I will not be afraid of anything. If God is on my side, how can anyone hurt me? The Eternal is on my side, a champion for my cause; so when I look at those who hate me, victory will be in sight. It is better to put your faith in the Eternal for your security than to trust in people.
> Psalm 118:6-8, The Voice Bible

PRAY

Father, in the Name of Jesus, I will arise as a mighty woman of God, using my voice to release my self-imposed limitations and break every limitation that the enemy has placed upon my life. Oh Lord, I thank You that You are an extraordinary God who accomplishes extraordinary things through me.
I pray this in Jesus' Name. Amen!

CHAPTER 11

Circle the Generations

Praying Mama: Alberta King, AKA Mama King

Alberta King, known as Mama King, worked hard to instill self-respect into her children. In an essay he wrote at Crozer Seminary, Martin Luther King, Jr., who was always close to his mother, wrote that she "was behind the scenes setting forth those motherly cares, the lack of which leaves a missing link in life." As a black woman raising black children in the 1950s, she's memorialized more for raising the most famous civil rights leader in history than her own activism.

— Mother of Martin Luther King, Jr.

Remember his covenant forever — the commitment he made to a thousand generations.

1 Chronicles 16:15, NLT

If I were to open your Bible, I'm sure I would see scripture promises you've circled to focus your attention on what you're believing God for. My Bible is filled with circled promises and dated when these promises are fulfilled. They serve as memorials to the faithfulness of God, His Word, and His covenant.

You don't have to feel qualified, nor fully understand the magnitude of the power generated when you circle God's covenant promises. However, it is imperative that you believe that God is for you. If you don't believe God is for you, you will find yourself going in circles with your prayer life.

Some people call circling promises, "prayer circles." I call mine Covenant Circles because I am in covenant with the Living God and His promises are for me and a thousand generations to come; that certainly includes my family and yours. In other words, "His covenant is without end" as it is promised.

> He is Jehovah our God: His judgments are in all the earth. He hath remembered his covenant forever, The word which he commanded to a thousand generations.
>
> Psalm 105:7-8, ASV

Much can be gleaned from the Native American culture. Recently, I attended a conference where a Native American Chieftain was the featured speaker. He began his session explaining what a circle means to the First Nation people. He said, "A circle, to the Native American people, always means **covenant** or **unity** because with a circle, there is no exit or entrance. You can't get out, and you can't get in. Once you're there, you're there. It's a circle that always exists."

Years ago, I read, *The Legend of Honi*. It verified the fact that I can be bold and ask God for the impossible. I want to share with you *The Legend of the Circle Maker*. Perhaps like me, it will challenge you to take your prayers to a new level. The legend reads as follows:

The Legend of the Circle Maker

It was the first century BC and a devastating drought threatened to destroy a generation, the generation before Jesus. The last of the Jewish prophets had died off nearly four centuries before. Miracles were such a distant memory that they seemed like a false memory. And God was nowhere to be heard. But there was one man, an eccentric sage who lived outside the walls of Jerusalem, who dared to pray anyway. His name was Honi. And even if the people could no longer hear God, he believed that God could still hear them. When rain is plentiful, it's an afterthought. During a drought, it's the only thought. And Honi was their only hope. Famous for his ability to pray for rain, it was on this day—the day—that Honi would earn his moniker.

With a six-foot staff in his hand, Honi began to turn like a math compass. His circular movement was rhythmical and methodical. Ninety degrees. One hundred and eighty degrees. Two hundred and seventy degrees. Three hundred and sixty degrees. He never looked up as the crowd looked on. After what seemed like hours, but had only been seconds, Honi stood inside the circle he had drawn. Then he dropped to his knees and raised his hands to heaven. With the authority of the prophet Elijah who called down fire from heaven, Honi called down rain.

"Lord of the Universe, I swear before your great name that I will not move from this circle until you have shown mercy upon your children."

The words sent a shudder down the spine of all who were within earshot that day. It wasn't just the volume of his voice. It was the authority of his tone. Not a hint of doubt. This prayer didn't originate in the vocal chords. Like water from an artesian well, the words flowed from the depth of his soul. His prayer was resolute yet humble; confident yet meek; expectant yet unassuming. Then it happened.

As his prayer ascended to the heavens, raindrops descended to the earth. An audible gasp swept across the thousands of congregants who had encircled Honi. Every head turned heavenward as the first raindrops parachuted from the sky, but Honi's head remained bowed. The people rejoiced over each drop, but Honi wasn't satisfied with a sprinkle. Still kneeling within the circle, Honi lifted his voice over the sounds of celebration.

"Not for such rain have I prayed, but for rain that will fill cisterns, pits, and caverns."

The sprinkle turned into such a torrential downpour that eyewitnesses said no raindrop was smaller than an egg in size. It rained so heavily and so steadily that the people fled to the Temple Mount to escape the flash floods. Honi stayed and prayed inside his protracted circle. Once more he refined his bold request.

"Not for such rain have I prayed, but for rain of Thy favor, blessing, and graciousness."

Then, like a well-proportioned sun shower on a hot and humid August afternoon, it began to rain calmly, peacefully. Each raindrop was a tangible token of God's grace. And they didn't just soak the skin; they soaked the spirit with faith. It would be forever remembered as the day. The day thunderclaps applauded the Almighty. The day puddle jumping became an act of praise. The day the legend of the circle maker was born. It had been difficult to believe the day before the day. The day after the day, it was impossible not to believe.

Honi was celebrated like a hometown hero by the people whose lives he had saved. But some within the Sanhedrin called the Circle Maker into question. A faction believed that drawing a circle and demanding rain dishonored God. Maybe it was those same members of the Sanhedrin who would criticize Jesus for healing a man's withered arm on the Sabbath a generation later. They threatened Honi with excommunication, but because the miracle could not be repudiated, Honi was ultimately honored for his act of prayerful bravado.

The prayer that saved a generation was deemed one of the most significant prayers in the history of Israel. The circle he drew in the sand became a sacred symbol.

And the legend of Honi the circle maker stands forever as a testament to the power of a single prayer to change the course of history.[1]

Praying Mama, God is still looking for Circle Makers, because Circle Makers are History Makers. History Makers are those who won't settle for less than what God promised for His covenant people, and have the boldness to ask for the impossible. I believe you are one of those who is bold enough to draw covenant circles in the sand, for the lives of the upcoming generations.

If God answered a single prayer of a man, and saved a generation from destruction, what is going to happen when an army of Spirit-filled mamas stand in unity and declare God's covenant promises over families, communities, and nations? Honi understood covenant and had no problem speaking to God as his father:

Because you are in covenant with God, you have a legal right to circle His everlasting promises and declare them over your seed.

Today I have given you the choice between life and death, between blessings and curses. Now I call on heaven and earth to witness the choice you make. Oh, that you would choose life, so that you and your descendants might live!

Deuteronomy 30:19, NLT

God is concerned about the peace of your children. He wants to bless you, your family, and the millennial generation of which they are a part. You must make a choice between life and death, blessings and curses, if you want your descendants to live the abundant life God has planned for them. This abundant life can

---

[1] To read more about Honi, see "The Deeds of the Sages," p. 201–203, in The Book of Legends. See also, Everyman's Talmud by Abraham Cohen, p. 277, and The Treatise Ta'anit of the Babylonian Talmud by Henry Malter, p. 270. NOTE: Honi the Circle Maker is sometimes referred to as Choni the Circle Maker, Honi Ha-Meaggel, and Onias the Rain Maker. Page | 8, © 2011 by Mark Batterson. You are permitted and encouraged to use this outline as the basis for your own preaching and teaching.

only come into fruition through God's Word, which is alive and active.

Circle the following covenant promise in your bible and boldly declare it over your children and grandchildren.

All thy children shall be taught of Jehovah, and great shall be the peace of thy children.

Isaiah 54:13, Darby

Make a stronger statement by making it personal:

All of my children _____NAME(S)_____ are taught of the Lord and great is the peace of my children _____NAME(S)_____.

That decree, prophetically speaking, is putting a covenant circle around your seed; they can't get out of the circle and nothing can get in the circle to cause them harm. It is also a form of binding them to the promises of God. The Word of God is Perfect, Alive and Powerful. His Word has proven itself time and time again in my life and the lives of my children.

The story in Mark 7:36 is a perfect example of a mama who knew the power of Jesus and asked Him for help on behalf of her daughter who was in an unbearable situation. Even though she wasn't a Jew, this mother knew Jesus could help her daughter who was caught in a web of impossibility. Perhaps this story best describes the condition of our present generation who have been labeled as cutters, deplorable, and without hope:

The woman was a Gentile, a Syrophoenician by birth. And she begged him to cast the demon out of her daughter.

Mark 7:26, ESV

J. C. Ryle comments:

The woman who came to our Lord, in the history now before us, must doubtless have been in deep affliction. She saw a beloved child possessed by an unclean spirit. She saw her in a condition in which no teaching could reach the mind, and no medicine could heal the body — a condition only one degree better than death itself. She hears of Jesus, and beseeches him to "cast forth the devil out of her daughter." She prays for one who could not pray for herself, and never rests till her prayer is granted.

By prayer she obtains the cure which no human means could obtain. Through the prayer of the mother, the daughter is healed. On her own behalf that daughter did not speak a word; but her mother spoke for her to the Lord, and did not speak in vain. Hopeless and desperate as her case appeared, she had a praying mother, and where there is a praying mother there is always hope.[1]

Praying Mamas, never forget you are God's conquering tribe that is bold enough to draw a covenant circle around this generation of young people and not relent until your prayers are granted. Our voice united can be the voice that saves the next generation.

> Truly I tell you, whatever you forbid and declare to be improper and unlawful on earth must be what is already forbidden in heaven, and whatever you permit and declare proper and lawful on earth must be what is already permitted in heaven. [19]Again I tell you, if two of you on earth agree (harmonize together, make a symphony together) about whatever [anything and everything] they may ask, it will come to pass and be done for them by My Father in heaven.
>
> Matthew 18:18-19; AMP

---

[1] J. C. Ryle's studylight.org, *Expository Thoughts on the Gospels*, Mark 7:24-30; 1859.

Drawing circles around God's promises might seem foreign to you or even foolish, but that's faith. One writer said, "Faith is the willingness to look foolish." We all know the story of Moses, we studied it in Sunday school. He must have felt and looked foolish when he went before Pharaoh and demanded him to let God's people go. How foolish do you think he looked when he lifted his staff over the Red Sea? Mamas, Moses's willingness to look foolish speaks for its self. The results? A generation was set free of Egypt's bondage and the Nation of Israel crossed the Red Sea on dry land.

Are you willing to take the risk of looking like you lack good sense? David, the shepherd boy, looked pretty pea-brained as he charged Goliath with only a sling shot for a weapon. The results of his bold faith was a dead giant with his head cut off. Giant killers are risk takers! If you don't take a risk you will probably forfeit the miracle for your family.

Praying Mamas, drawing circles is not the same as giving you a mastercard to get what you want from God. Drawing circles is glorifying God by circling the promises He has available for you, His covenant child, your children and grandchildren. These covenant promises are good to a thousand generations. They are unending.

Let's regress here and make a short statement about God's covenant for your family. God has a lot of good things in store for you and the generations to come. These benefits are all yours and your family because you are God's covenant child through Jesus Christ His Son. Jesus is the Living Word and the written Word. In the Bible are His Covenant Promises based on His word of honor:

> In the same way, when God wanted to confirm His promise as true and unchangeable, He swore an oath to the heirs of that promise. So God has given us two unchanging things: *His promise and His oath*.
>
> Hebrews 6:17, 18, The Voice Bible

Many times, we think of a covenant in a negative sense, as something we must do or suffer unpleasant consequences. To the contrary, the New Covenant ratified by the Blood of Jesus is positive. When you enter into God's new covenant, His many promises become yours not for you only, but also for your children and your grandchildren. By faith, God wants you to put your family into a circle of His promises to protect them from impending harm. They can't get out and nothing can get in to cause harm, but you have to place them in your circle.

Praying Mama, you possess a power beyond that of a king on his throne. The power of a mother is not to be deemed unimportant. Just ask a mother bear. Your prayers will turn you into a ferocious mama who shapes the destinies of your children, grandchildren, and generations that follow. Your prayers never die. They live on in the lives of future generations for whom you have interceded. In the old western movies when an attack came against their families, they circled their wagons to form a barrier between the enemy and their family. Praying Mamas, **"It's time to circle the wagons!"**

NOTE:
Martin Luther King Jr. (January 15, 1929 – April 4, 1968) was an American Baptist minister and activist who became the most visible spokesperson and leader in the civil rights movement from 1954 until his death in 1968. His mother, Alberta King, was killed while playing the organ in church six years after his assassination.

סֶלָה

SELAH
PAUSE–PONDER–PRAY

PAUSE
If you want God to do something new, you can't keep doing the same old thing. You have to dare to be different, and that includes praying bold prayers and expecting them to be answered.

PONDER
Men and women of the Bible were not super saints. Honi and Elijah were not super saints, they were people just like you and me. They received answers to their prayers because they put their faith in God, trusting in His character and His Word. The Bible makes that very clear:

> The earnest prayer of a righteous person has great power and produces wonderful results. Elijah was as human as we are, and yet when he prayed earnestly that no rain would fall, none fell for three and a half years! Then, when he prayed again, the sky sent down rain and the earth began to yield its crops.
>
> James 5:16-18

Ask yourself the following question: *Do I think of the Word of God as being alive and active on my behalf, or is reading the Bible just a religious practice to me?*

Ponder and write the answer to the next question: *Do I believe in the trustworthiness of the One to whom I am praying? Do I believe that God will keep His Word and answer my prayer like He did for Elijah and the Circle Maker?*

PRAY

Father, I thank You that I have the power to release life wherever I go. I will not let fear hold me back. I pray for boldness and courage to believe that You will keep Your Word and answer my prayer like You did for Elijah and the Circle Maker.

I pray this in Jesus' Name. Amen!

CHAPTER 12

Don't Ring The Bell

Praying Mama: Morrow Graham

Speaking on Mother's Day in 2003, Mr. Graham told the audience in San Diego that his mother was a farm woman. "She and my father didn't have much education... but my mother was a woman of God. She always had devotions with us, she always prayed with us, she always loved us, and did so many things for us. Of all the people I have ever known, she had the greatest influence on me. I am sure one reason that the Lord has directed and safeguarded me, as well as Ruth and the children, through the years was the prayers of my mother and father. She and my father, when I was in Bible school, would go up to a room upstairs and kneel down every morning at 10 o'clock to pray for their son in Bible school."

— Mother of Billy Graham

Then I, God, will burst all confinements and lead them out into the open. They'll follow their King. I will be out in front leading them.

Micah 2:13; MSG

I will reiterate it again, "We are not alone in the battle for the forthcoming generations." God is fighting with us and for us. We must never forget the promise in His Word, Romans 8:31: "If God is for us, who or what can stand against us?"
We need not fear; King Jesus is on our side and leading us into victory on every front. Jesus is both King and Lord: He reigns and He rules.

The Eternal is with me so I will not be afraid of anything. If God is on my side, how can anyone hurt me?

Psalm 118:6, The Voice Bible

Praying Mamas, Jesus is getting ready to burst all the imprisonments off our families, and He is going to use YOU to get the job done. Bobby Conner said this about our families:
Our families can be a place of comfort or a place of anxiety, especially concerning our children. Someone once said:

"A mother is only as happy as her saddest child, which is true for fathers also. We all carry loved ones in our hearts; their battles become our battles, adding stress and anxiety to the load we already carry." [1]

God does not want us to be stressed about this end-time war. He has given us all we need to win the conflict between good and evil. As already stated, He is on your side! You will never face a single battle alone; it doesn't matter how large or how small. The Lord is concerned about every detail of your family, as well as the condition of your community, city, state and nation. The battle belongs to God, and He gives us breakthrough in every violent skirmish we face with the enemy.

Several weeks ago, out of nowhere, the enemy of doubt hit me hard. At the time I was about 90 percent finished with this manuscript, the enemy began to challenge me with insulting remarks, reminding me of all the wonderful books already written about women rising in the last days. For sure he mocked the title of this book, *Praying Mamas, God's End-Time Manifesto;* declaring it to be the most idiotic title anyone could ever come

---

[1] Bobby Conner, *Shepherd's Rod*, Volume XVII 2012, Kindle Locations, 592-594.

up with. The war was not against me alone; it was over Praying Mamas, and their role in God's end-time army.

The enemy, Satan, knows you are going to become a Holy terror to his kingdom of darkness, and he is doing everything he can to stop you. I was in a Salvation Army store at the time of that epic encroachment of my mind. I was looking for antiques when suddenly I experienced an epiphany, a visitation from God. He drew my attention to a small tin box with a latch on it. All four sides of this tin had depictions of women preparing for war. The lid pictured a woman flexing her muscles with the caption in bold letters, WE CAN DO IT. The back side showed a woman at work. The text said, "Women in the war, WE CAN'T WIN WITHOUT THEM." One side showed a woman saluting and her brief statement was, "Yes, Sir, I am here." The other side read "These women are doing their bit." How is that for confirmation of this book? Women volunteering for war; confirmation in a Salvation Army establishment!

The war over our families will not end during this life. I know that's not a great report, but the good news is "WE WIN" if we don't give up when the battle gets tough. The famous quote of Joseph P. Kennedy is applicable here:

"When the going gets tough, the tough get going."[1]

In Praying Mama terms, it means when the war becomes difficult, the end-time army of resilient Mamas fights even harder to meet the challenge. As an army, we must gear up for the battles ahead and be totally saturated in God's Word.

Be prepared. You're up against far more than you can handle on your own. Take all the help you can get; every weapon God has issued. When it's

---

[1] https://www.brainyquote.com/authors/joseph_p_kennedy. Accessed April 1, 2019.

all over but the shouting, you'll still be on your feet. Truth, righteousness, peace, faith, and salvation are more than words. Learn how to apply them. You'll need them throughout your life. God's Word is an indispensable weapon. In the same way, prayer is essential in this ongoing warfare. Pray hard and long. Pray for your brothers and sisters. Keep your eyes open. Keep each other's spirits up so that no one falls behind or drops out.

Ephesians 6:13-18, MSG

In this passage, Paul gives us instructions how to remain tough in battle and fight with the Word of God and prayer. He reminds us that God's Word is "an indispensable weapon," and that prayer is a necessary key for the ongoing warfare we are engaged in. It is of vital importance that we stay saturated in God's Word in order to be successful in warfare.

My grandparents raised cattle for their income. I often watched the cows as they chewed their cud. Little did I know those unpretentious cows were giving me a prophetic portrait of meditating on God's Word. Here is what Richard Foster says about ruminating God's Word:

"Have you ever watched a cow chew its cud? This unassuming animal will fill its stomach with grass and other food. Then it settles down quietly and, through a process of regurgitation, reworks what it has received, slowly moving its mouth in the process. In this way it is able to fully assimilate what it has previously consumed, which is then transformed into rich, creamy milk. So, it is with meditative prayer. The truth being meditated upon passes from the mouth into the mind and down into the heart, where through quiet rumination — regurgitation, if you will — it produces in the person praying a loving, faith-filled response. When we meditate on Scripture allowing the Spirit to breathe upon the written logos it becomes rhema in our spirit, bringing with it the creative power of heaven and once again the Word becomes flesh as He dwells in us through the transforming power of His Word. Meditation is not so much about what you read, but more about what you chew.[1]

We need to have a steady diet of God's Word, which will, in turn, give us strength and strategy for war. When we meditate, eat, and digest the Word of God, it transforms the written words into a life-giving force that quickens us and causes us to become Holy terrors against Satan's kingdom.

Praying Mamas, chew on this for a while, "You have a two-edged sword at your disposal anytime you come against the spirits of darkness" (Hebrews 4:12, AMP). The Epistle to the Hebrews refers to the Word of God as a Sword:

The Word of God is living and active and full of power [making it operative, energizing, and effective]. It is sharper than any two-edged sword.

Hebrews 4:12, AMP

For years, I studied and taught on the topic of the Word of God, a sword that cuts two ways. I never fully understood the significance of the two edges until I read Rick Renner's Greek commentary of God's Word being a two-edged sword:

The phrase "two-edged" is taken from the Greek word *distomos* and is unquestionably one of the oddest words in the entire New Testament. Why is it so odd? Because it is a compound of the

[1] Richard Foster, *Prayer*, **http://kingswayal.com/writings/view/60-Eating-the-Book-Becoming-the-Word**. Accessed 3/28/2019.

word *di*, meaning two, and the word *stomos*, which is the Greek word for one's mouth. Thus, when these two words are compounded into one, *distomos*, they describe something that is two-mouthed![1]

Let's break this down. First, that word came out of the mouth of God, then it came out of your mouth! When it came out of your mouth, it became a sharp, "two-edged" or literally, a "two-mouthed" word. One edge of this sword came into existence when the Word initially proceeded out of God's mouth. The second edge of this sword was added when the Word of God proceeded out of *your* mouth! The Word of God remains a one-bladed sword when it comes out of God's mouth and drops into your heart but is never released from your own mouth by faith.

That supernatural Word simply lies dormant in your heart, never becoming the two-edged sword God designed it to be. You must get the Word from your spirit, into your head and out of your mouth. Something happens in the realm of the Spirit when you finally rise up and begin to speak forth that Word. The moment it comes out of your mouth, it becomes the "two-mouthed sword" described in the Scriptures. That's when demons start to tremble in terror! God's Word has the power to defeat every adversity we face in our life and in the lives of our children. It is a mighty, sharp, two-edged sword that releases His power when we declare it out of our mouth. The more we use the Sword of the Spirit, the sharper it gets.

It is time to sharpen our swords and go to war for our righteous seed. In other words, we need to study and meditate on God's Word for impartation as opposed to just reading the Word for information. When Jesus was in the war over His Divine destiny, He used the same sword that is available to us today, The Sword of The Spirit. With confidence He wielded the sword, putting an end to the tyranny of the enemy. Satan was

---

[1] Rick Renner, *Sparkling Gems*: From The Greek, Harrison House Publishers, p. 109.

trying to lure Him away from His Divine destiny. He knew if Jesus completed what His Father commissioned him to do, it would spoil the kingdom of his principalities and powers.

Jesus knew the power of the Word. He declared, "It is written and forever remains written, Man shall not live by bread alone, but by every Word that comes out of the mouth of God" (Matthew 4:4, AMP) The conclusion of the matter is, the enemy had to flee, but he never gave up. He began strategizing for his next battle against Jesus. I like this statement; "The Word works for those who work the Word." The late James Ryle said it like this, *Get in the Word until the Word gets in you.*

We must stand in this hour, clothed in the full Armor of God, with our two-edged sword in hand; ready for the next battle over the generations to come. I cannot say it any better than the lyrics to this song, *Break Every Chain:*

There's an army rising up
To Break every chain-Break every chain
Break every chain (2x)
There is Power in the name of Jesus
There is Power in the name of Jesus
There is Power in the name of Jesus
To Break every chain
Break every chain
Break every chain [1]

The Father has commissioned You to be part of an Army that's rising up to break the fetter placed on this millennial generation. With one voice we must declare that the strongholds of drug addiction, suicide, depression, and commercial sex trading of our sons and daughters will be broken in Jesus' Name.

The enemy knows his victory ends when we as an army of Praying Mamas make the commitment to fight for our babies. And when we do… the victory begins. Praying Mamas, if you

---

[1] **https://en.wikipedia.org/wiki/Break_Every_Chain**. Accessed 3/28/2019.

want to change the course of generations to come, *Don't Ever Ring The Bell!*

I will close this chapter, with Admiral McRaven's challenge to the 2014 graduating class of the University of Texas. He ended his commencement speech with the following statement.

> Finally, in SEAL training there is a bell, a brass bell that hangs in the center of the compound for all the students to see. All you have to do to quit is ring the bell. Ring the bell, and you no longer have to wake up at five o'clock. Ring the bell, and you no longer have to do the freezing cold swims. Ring the bell, and you no longer have to do the runs, the obstacle course, the PT, and you no longer have to endure the hardships of training. Just ring the bell.
> **If you want to change the world, don't ever, ever ring the bell.**[1]

[1] William H. McRaven, *Make Your Bed*, Grand Central Publishing. Kindle Edition. P. 124.

סֶלָה

SELAH
PAUSE—PONDER—PRAY

PAUSE
Glory! Glory! Hallelujah! His Truth Is Marching On!

The Battle Hymn of the Republic
Mine eyes have seen the glory of the coming of the Lord;
He is trampling out the vintage where the grapes of wrath are stored;
He hath loosed the fateful lightning of His terrible swift sword:
His truth is marching on.

Glory! Glory! Hallelujah!
Glory! Glory! Hallelujah!
Glory! Glory! Hallelujah!
His truth is marching on.

I have read His fiery gospel writ in rows of burnished steel:
"As ye deal with my condemners, so with you My grace shall deal";
Let the Hero, born of woman, crush the serpent with his heel, Since God is marching on.

He has sounded forth the trumpet that shall never call retreat;
He is sifting out the hearts of men before His judgment-seat;
Oh, be swift, my soul, to answer Him! Be jubilant, my feet!
Our God is marching on.[1]

---

[1] https://www.civilwarheritagetrails.org/civil-war-music/battle-hymn-of-the-republic.html. Accessed 3/28/2019.

PONDER

I encourage you to go online and listen to this Battle Hymn. Journal the times when you were on the verge of giving up and how the Holy Spirit gave you the strength and determination to rise above the difficulties you were facing.

PRAY

Pray and decree these verses and chorus until you feel jubilant and swift to answer His call. Our God is marching on! His Truth is marching on!

EPILOGUE

As I write the conclusion of this book, I want to remind you of the fact that your existence in this time of history is proof enough that you have something to give to the generations. Because you are unique, no one else can fulfill what God called you to do.

I have been alive on planet Earth for more than 78 years and have felt the effects of many wars. However, in my lifetime I have never experienced a more challenging time than the hour in which we live. Our culture seems to have lost all sense of direction and all the values of life. The war over our children and the next generation is the most horrific war I have ever seen or been involved in. The late Myles Munroe said it so brilliantly:

> History shows that the value of life decreases, and the quality of existence diminishes when a generation loses it sense of destiny and purpose. A quick glance at our current world exposes a sad picture that demands our attention. We preserve nature, for example, but kill babies. We build solid houses but cannot construct lasting homes. We are smarter but not wiser, bigger but not stronger. We know more but understand less, and we live longer but enjoy life less fully. We write more books but fail to take the time to read them. We go faster but get nowhere, conquer space but cannot conquer our habits, protect whales but abuse our children, go to the moon but wander far from home, and flirt with fantasy to avoid reality.[1]

I want to share with you what was the catalyst for this book. Several months ago, my husband and I simultaneously shared a

---

[1] Myles Munroe, In Pursuit of Purpose, Destiny Image Publisher Inc., Introduction.

disturbing occurrence. It was a phenomenon that had no logical explanation. We were both awakened from a sound sleep by the most haunting scream we have ever heard. At one and the same time, we sat up in the bed. Looking at each other, we realized it was a scream of distress, and it was coming from our oldest, great granddaughter, Jaedyn. Immediately anxiety tried to grip our hearts. I quickly came against fear and concluded there was no eminent danger. Our granddaughter, Jessica, without fail, prays Psalm 91 over her children every day when they are in route to school. She puts them under the Blood of Jesus and the shadow of the Almighty, claiming the protective promises found in Psalm 91.

For several weeks I pondered about the purpose and why that happened to us. I asked the Lord for clarification as to why my husband and I heard that unforgettable, haunting scream of our great granddaughter. Then one day during my prayer time, the Holy Spirit spoke clearly to me about the incident. He explained to me it was a wakeup call from her generation asking for our help. He knows I'm like a mama bear when it comes to one of my children, grandchildren, or my spiritual children being hurt or endangered. Let me tell you, He certainly got my attention by using a scream from my great granddaughter.

The Holy Spirit likened her scream to THE SHOT THAT WAS HEARD AROUND THE WORLD, which was the beginning of the American Revolutionary War in 1775. He emphasized that the *Jaedyn Scream* needs to be heralded around the world, calling attention to the violent war that is currently raging over our children. He reminded me, while we were comfortably sleeping, young girls and boys were being sold as sex slaves to bring gratification to deranged men and women of this crazed society. I was also reminded of young cutters, who cut gashes in their flesh with the hopes of escaping the painful situation they find themselves in, with no way out or a place to go. It didn't stop there. He reminded me that drug abuse, depression, and suicide are an epidemic in our society, even in the younger generation my great granddaughter's age.

Praying Mamas, it is time to rise and do something about all these horrendous assignments against the generations. I didn't share all of this to make you fearful. I shared it with the hope of awakening you to the fact our culture is sick, and our children need our help.

This whole book has been written because of that scream asking for help, and the mandate given to mothers to arise as a united army — armed and ready for battle.

> The time for the lone wolf is over. Gather yourselves! Banish the word struggle from your attitude and your vocabulary. All that we do now must be done in a sacred manner and in celebration. We are the ones we've been waiting for.
>
> — the Hopi Nation Oraibi, Arizona

As you read the closing pages of this book, it is my prayer that something will arise within you and cause you to become who you are, a Holy terror to the kingdom of darkness. I can't think of a higher calling than to be an intercessor for this generation and a terrorist against Satan's kingdom.

I realize I am in the winter season of my life. I fully intend to help amass an army of Praying Mamas. My plans are to have Praying Mama boot camps, teaching warfare tactics to those who are not afraid to go to the enemy's camp, taking back what has been stolen from them, their family, community, and nation. It is my full intent to stir up the gifts in these mamas that have laid dormant for years. The enemy has tried to make these mighty warriors feel inferior because of their past and social standing. Many are in bondage over the fact that they had an abortion, while others were infringed upon when they were young, taking away their innocence. I could go on with a list as to why we feel ashamed and ineffective in the Kingdom of God. Mothers, God's Grace is big enough to cover abortions or any other thing the enemy has hit you with.

Praying Mamas, it's time to move on. We're an army and it's time to take the land. There comes a time in all of our lives when we need to take stock of what was, what is, and what can be. Don't hold on to stuff that prevents you from becoming who you can be.

We must leave a legacy of prayer to the next generation and teach them how to war. They can learn, and we must teach them by example. If we want them to be Holy terrors to Satan's kingdom of darkness, then we need to show them how it is done. This Tswana proverb speaks volumes:

> The young bird does not crow until it hears the old ones.[1]

Let me remind you, quitting when the going gets tough is not an option. God has placed you in the Kingdom for such a time as this. Admiral McRaven said this to the 2014, University of Texas graduating class, "Never, Ever Quit. If you quit, you will regret it for the rest of your life. Quitting never makes anything easier."

Mamas, I pray blessings upon you and declare that your generation has twice the anointing as mine, and you will finish what my generation started. A finishing anointing is coming upon you. Never forget:

> You are God's End-time Manifesto, and you are anointed with an anointing of excessive strength!
>
> Psalm 92:10

If you feel you need healing of the past, it's not as difficult as the enemy would have you believe. Simply pray the prayer below. If need be, write a Personal Manifesto and declare scriptures over yourself every day. Your generation is the one He is depending

---

[1] https://quotescover.com/topics/Tswana+Proverb.

on. He can't do it without you! Let's be unified as we declare, "Oh Lord, do it again!"

A prayer for those who need healing of the past:

> Lord Jesus, I open my heart, and let You into places of hurt and shame I may never have opened to anyone else before. I surrender my anger and bitterness and submit to Your process of deliverance. Take from me now those snares that have been planted by the enemy of my soul and replace them with the loving fellowship of Your Comforter, the Holy Spirit, who drives away all my fear. I praise Your Holy Name, Lord God!
>
> I forgive completely all who have wounded me and release them to Your abundant blessing that they too might be converted into children of the Kingdom. Thank You for the overflow of Your healing and grace. I worship You with all my heart, dear Lord. In Jesus' Name I pray, Amen.

About Nancy and Her
PRAYING MAMA Journey

Nancy is without question the purest Biblical example of a virtuous woman, dearest wife, excellent Mother, extraordinary Grandmother and Great grandmother that our Heavenly Father ever created. From her early childhood to this very moment, she has maintained a life totally surrendered and fully committed to be a true daughter to our Heavenly father, His only Son Jesus Christ, and His Precious Holy Spirit. She and her husband of 58 years of marriage, have been in full time ministry all of their married Life together. Nancy is co-founder of Harvest International Ministries, Inc.

Over a span of almost six decades she has served in many areas of Christian service such as Ordained Minister, CoPastor, Missionary, Woman's Director for prayer and intercession and has directed and spoken at women's conferences over the past many years. For several years, she served as Dean of Women at Christ For The Nations in Dallas, Texas.

With all of this history of service for the Kingdom of Heaven, absolutely, no doubt, her most outstanding work for the King of Glory has been as a PRAYING MAMA. It has sustained her personal life, and that of her entire family both biological and spiritual. There is absolutely no doubt what so ever that her life of unwavering, sustained daily prayer to her Father in Heaven is the fundamental and foundational dynamic of preserving of such an admirable life of service for Kingdom of God. Trust me, I know, I'm her husband,

Samuel L. Brassfield.

Find Nancy at

http://www.prayingmamas.org/

You can also follow her @PrayingMamasInternational on both Facebook and Instagram.

RESOURCES

If you would like to learn more about how to be an effective Praying Mama, visit Nancy's website at:

http://www.prayingmamas.org/

You will also find information there on how to invite Nancy to set up a Praying Mamas BootCamp at your church or women's group and help train a whole generation of women (and men)to fight for their families, stand on God's unfailing word, and see Him move mightily on their behalf!

PRAYING MAMA BootCamp Training

Email: orders@prayingmamas.org

Mailing address: 333 County Road Bertram, Texas 78605

Additionally on her website you will find items such as Praying Mamas t-shirts, aprons, STRENGTH OF THE OX Anointing Oil, Workbooks and Study Guides and lots of helpful articles and stories to build your faith!

Visit **www.prayingmamas.org** today!

Related Books Highly Recommended By Nancy

Each of the books below will help you continue your journey as a Praying Mama and will teach you powerful tools and things you must learn if you are going to be a powerful Woman of Prayer and Fellowship with The Lord.

- *How to Write A Covenant* by Brenda Zintcraff This book is a simple guide on how to write a covenant and watch God's word come to pass in your life. Brenda, as a young mother some thirty-six years ago, perceived that her prayers seemed to be bouncing off the ceiling. One night, a revelation of how to write a covenant captured her soul. Hebrews 4:12 opened her eyes to the ALIVE and ACTIVE Word of God and gave her insight on how to change history and the lives of her family. Through covenants, she has seen her family step into the full purpose of God for their lives. She has seen destinies change and continues to see history made through the writings of covenants.

- *The Pleasure Of His Company* by Dutch Sheets Learn from Dutch Sheets as he shares his life lessons for cultivating an intimate relationship with God. This book reveals a simple practice or biblical mindset that will help draw you away from the noise of life and into the Lord's peaceful presence.

- *The Kentucky Traveler* By Ricky Skaggs Ricky Skaggs, the music legend who revived modern bluegrass music, gives a warm, honest, one-of-a-kind memoir of forty years in music—along with a bevy of personal snapshots of his musical heroes and his personal walk of faith.

- *The Praying Mamas Workbook and Study Guide* By Nancy Brassfield (coming soon —check our website for release date)

Made in the USA
Monee, IL
23 January 2021